MR E.G. LIGHTBODY, MACC LI?? TV
MACC CHES. 43 15JUN
99

£2.00

19

'ENEMY SUBJECT'

LIFE IN A JAPANESE INTERNMENT CAMP 1943–45

PEGGY ABKHAZI

EDITED BY S.W. JACKMAN

FOREWORD BY

J.G. BALLARD

ALAN SUTTON PUBLISHING LIMITED

First published in 1981 by Sono Nis Press, Canada

First published in the United Kingdom in 1995 by
Alan Sutton Publishing Ltd · Phoenix Mill · Far Thrupp · Stroud
Gloucestershire

British Library Cataloguing in Publication Data

A catalogue record for this book is available from the British
Library.

ISBN 0-7509-0958-7

Printed in Great Britain by
Alden Press, Oxford and Northampton.

ALS?

to Nico

Portrait of Timmy

CONTENTS

7   Foreword

9   Editor's Introduction

21   First Journal
December 8th, 1941 to February 3rd, 1942

41   Waiting for Internment – Editor

47   Second Journal
March 4th, 1943 to September 12th, 1945

139   Postscript

141   Appendix

ILLUSTRATIONS

LILIAN SCHLEE, *Portrait of Timmy* and
My Corner of the Hut

DEIRDRE FEE, all other illustrations

FOREWORD

J. G. BALLARD

All the sights and smells of Lunghua camp rush through the pages of Peggy Abkhazi's remarkable diary, as if a window had suddenly opened in the small room that I shared with my father, mother and sister in G Block fifty years ago. Reading '*Enemy Subject*' I feel a stronger sense of returning to the camp than I did when revisiting Lunghua in 1988. Everything is here: the stench, the boredom, the fierce winter cold and stifling summers, the moody Japanese guards and equally unpredictable fellow internees.

Peggy Pemberton-Carter, as she was in Lunghua, taught me French in the camp school, and I wish that I could remember her in person. Her diary suggests a woman of determined character, as critical of herself as she is of the other prisoners who share her dormitory hut. She seems always aware of the paradoxes that govern so much of human behaviour. In Lunghua she found that affectation of any kind was soon stripped away, revealing the true personality beneath the veneer, but also that 'the liars are often generous, and the greedy ones are very clean . . .'.

The portrait she paints of Lunghua coincides almost exactly with my own memories, though our perspectives were very different. I was a boy in my early teens, and she a mature woman without the responsibilities of husband or children. I assume that this gave her the freedom to remain detached from the often desperate life around her, and the mental space to reflect on the lessons that internment taught about human nature and its response to boredom, hunger and the enforced company of those one detests.

Readers will notice that the diary's tone changes during the years, from the confidence of the opening entries to the creeping depression that dominates the last year of the war. It is important

7

to remember, as one tries to visualize the prisoners' feelings at the time, that no one in Lunghua expected the war to end in August 1945. My own parents, and the adults I met in the camp, all assumed that the war would last at least another year, if not longer, a grim prospect as the food rations fell and people succumbed in greater numbers to malaria. I have always been aware that my parents had far harsher memories of internment than the cheerful ones I carried with me from Lunghua.

Few British civilians, compared with those of our Allies, endured enemy captivity during the Second World War, and 'Enemy Subject' is an invaluable record of the courage and stoicism displayed by almost all the British men and women interned in Lunghua during those frequently painful but always extraordinary years.

Editor's Introduction

S. W. JACKMAN

In the twentieth century many people have suffered imprisonment because of political beliefs, racial origins or war. In the last instance many were soldiers who were captured in the course of fighting; while others were interned because they were unfortunate enough to be caught when military forces of occupation took control of their lives. History recounts, both in the present day and in the past, how people coped with the adversities posed by these disruptive and frequently terrible conditions. Most of the tales are ones of unmitigated horror, since they seem to have attracted the attention of the world. Inhuman imprisonment, torture, starvation and mass murder are common. However, there are fewer reports of the experiences of those who were victims, but whose distress was more muted and less violent. To have lived under an army or occupation, even if the soldiers were not necessarily brutal, is to have experienced a sense of demoralization because one is cut off from the mainstream of one's experience. Internment is a more severe version of the same experience. Relatively few people have been able to keep a coherent account of what they felt and what happened to them while incarcerated because authority was, in general, opposed to such a record. Peggy Pemberton-Carter Abkhazi was one of those rare individuals who did manage to record in some detail her life under such circumstances. She required courage and fortitude to write regularly; weariness and lassitude overtake the average diarist under the best of circumstances and she was living under conditions that do not normally encourage such literary endeavour. One rarely has the opportunity to know in such detail the daily round of internment. This journal is, therefore, a somewhat unusual historical document describing as it does the very particular position of the civilian confronted with the military might of an invading army.

Peggy Pemberton-Carter Abkhazi was born in Shanghai in December 1902, the only child of William James Blaylock Carter and his wife Mabel Carter. William Carter was an architect who had gone to China at the turn of the century where he worked for Lester, Johnson & Morriss, a firm which had designed a number of large buildings in the European section of Shanghai. The young architect was an attractive and agreeable young man, good at games, and popular with a wide circle of society, but at the same time somewhat feckless and irresponsible. Despite these flaws in his character he was well regarded by his professional colleagues and thought to have a promising future. Relatively little is known of his family antecedents and, except for a sister, he seems to have had no other relatives. Mabel Blackburn Carter on the other hand was a product of a more traditional background; her father, her three sisters and at least three brothers lived in West Kirby in Lancashire. The lives of the Carters were varied and agreeable with little heed needing to be paid to the more dreary and humdrum aspects of the domestic world because of a retinue of Chinese servants. Even the arrival of a child in the household made little change; an amah (Chinese nurse) was readily available to care for the little girl.

Mabel Carter seems to have been happy enough in Shanghai but by 1905 it was discovered that the climate and situation were unsuitable, and that continued residence in China would be deleterious to her health. It was decided that she and her daughter should return to England for a time in the hopes that with careful nursing she might recover. Mother and daughter went to West Kirby but, sadly, Mabel Carter's state did not improve and shortly afterwards she died.

Her three-year-old child was now destined to live for a time with her grandfather and his unmarried sons and daughters. It was to be a somewhat lonely six months for her as her older relations, while never cruel, tended to disregard her. They had their own lives and their own interests; she was essentially an outsider. For one thing, the age difference was substantial and nobody appeared to be willing to do much to bring her into the family circle. She was not neglected — food and clothing were more than adequate — but she was not thought to be very significant. Her immediate needs were supplied, but her future was uncertain. Her maternal relations were prepared to do their duty but it seemed they did so without much enthusiasm.

A change in her existence ensued when her father's only sister, Polly Nicholson, offered to take the child into her house. Aunt Polly was a widow with one daughter named Daisy who was close in age to her cousin. This was thought to be a splendid solution to the problem and the three-year-old girl joined her widowed aunt at Bolton-le-Sands. Some time later the *ménage* moved to Lancaster.

William Carter sent money to his sister to help support the household. However, he too had begun to suffer from ill health and his general condition rapidly deteriorated. He was much concerned for the welfare of his daughter and to alleviate his worries two friends in Shanghai agreed to become her guardians should this be necessary. Shortly afterwards William Carter died and to the consternation of his friends and family, it was found that his affairs were in chaos and that he was unfortunately without assets. The guardians found themselves charged with a very real responsibility and without any means of fulfilling their obligations.

To resolve the situation Thomas and Florence Pemberton decided to adopt the orphan. They were a childless and wealthy couple who had been acquainted with William and Mabel Carter. The legal guardians were vastly relieved, and Polly Nicholson in England agreed when she too learned of her brother's insolvency, while the child's maternal grandfather offered no objections.

The Pembertons were a somewhat odd couple. Thomas Pemberton, who had established himself in Shanghai about 1863, was twenty-four years older than his wife. He was quite affluent and successful. Florence Pemberton, a handsome woman looking very much like Lady Randolph Churchill, and with all of her style and *élan*, had initially been a governess and companion, but she had attracted the attention of the middle-aged bachelor Thomas Pemberton and they were married in 1893.

Having resolved to adopt their late friend's daughter the Pembertons decided that the sensible course of action was to return to England themselves to collect her. This seemed easier than hiring some woman to bring her out to them. Moreover, they had apparently contemplated leaving Shanghai for a time at least to make a home for themselves elsewhere and the two projects could be combined.

Upon their arrival in England in 1907 they immediately went to Lancaster. Fortunately, Thomas and Florence Pemberton were delighted with the child and the latter, now used to sudden changes

11

in her existence, was not at all unhappy to go with them. For her a new and very much happier life was to begin.

The first sign of change was that she ceased to be called Marjorie. She was now named Peggy Pemberton. It was as Peggy Pemberton that she was to be known for the next twenty-five years. Subsequently the surname, Carter, was added to that of Pemberton. Very quickly Thomas and Florence Pemberton took a house and established themselves in that late Edwardian world of middle-class comfort their wealth and position permitted. Until 1918, when Thomas Pemberton died, there was little change in the family's way of life. Their adopted daughter was given the conventional education of the day, showing a particular aptitude for music, she was to become an accomplished pianist. Her parents paid for excellent instruction and it seemed as if she might have a career as a professional concert artist. This did not occur and she had to content herself with the role of the talented amateur, but music as an avocation rather than as a profession was to give her much pleasure.

Following Thomas Pemberton's demise at the end of the First World War, his widow and daughter began an existence that was essentially peripatetic. They travelled extensively in style and comfort, residing in no one place for any lengthy period; sometimes they remained for only a few weeks, sometimes for several months. In the early 1920's they were in Paris where they became acquainted with a young Georgian Prince named Nicholas Abkhazi who was studying at the Ecole des Sciences Politiques. He and Peggy Pemberton became good friends, taking walks in the Bois de Boulogne, visiting museums and attending concerts. They had many interests in common but for the moment they were fated to separate.

After living in Paris, Florence Pemberton and her daughter moved again, and one hotel succeeded another. Life consisted of packing and unpacking, enjoying the cultural scene of each new place but being essentially rootless. Constant travel, no matter how luxurious, ultimately becomes tedious; when one has been almost everywhere there seems little that is new anywhere to be savoured and enjoyed. In an attempt to alleviate the situation, Florence Pemberton made a decision; she would go back to Shanghai, a place which she remembered as being delightful; the less agreeable aspects had been conveniently forgotten and the international community, in recollection at least, was lively and engaging. Moreover, one could live in a style and fashion that had become increasingly difficult in Europe after 1918. The foreign residents in Shanghai and elsewhere in China could still have all of the pleasures that made the Edwardian era a halcyon period for those with money.

Peggy Pemberton and her mother established themselves in a handsome and agreeable residence. They were to remain together in Shanghai until Florence Pemberton's death in 1938; thereafter Peggy Pemberton-Carter, as she was now called, was totally without family obligations and responsibilities. She was financially independent and was able to fashion her life exactly to suit herself. She continued to live in the penthouse which she had shared with her mother; she was well cared for by a faithful staff, and her circle of friends was totally compatible. As she was to say later, "for the Europeans and the Americans, Shanghai was a sort of 'Never-never Land of Extra-territoriality' where riots, rebellions, civil wars could (and did) rage within sight and sound of the city," but those "Extra-territorial Rights" were ever present as a protection. The British, French and American authorities, backed up by small naval and military establishments, ensured safety. Aside from the occasional inconvenience caused by a passing army under its war-lord, there was no possibility of real danger, no significant hardship, no likelihood of financial disaster and no chance of the loss of property. Nothing had ever happened to those blessed beings with "Extra-territorial Rights," and, as far as could be imagined, nothing ever would disturb the pace of their lives. Against such sanguine expectations, and despite the military activities and successes of the Japanese which increasingly threatened the survival of the Chinese Republic, people who were in Shanghai had no incentive to depart.

To individuals like Peggy Pemberton-Carter any move had become more or less unthinkable. For her Shanghai was somehow where she belonged; although of British nationality, she had never really lived in England since she had become an adult. Moreover, her youth had been passed in almost constant travel with "home" being a series of hotel suites. Like many of her compatriots who resided in China, she became particularly attached to the country and to its people. The place had taken possession of her.

In addition, her staff had become a sort of family with its own sense of dependency upon her. With the devoted service they provided, came a mutual feeling of responsibility. Her Number One Boy named Li had been devoted to Florence Pemberton and had cared for her extremely faithfully during her illness; clearly, he could not simply be abandoned. Li's daughter, Ah Ching, who had recovered from tuberculosis because of her father's employers ability

13

to provide her with proper medical care, was convinced that she "belonged" to her young mistress. She was on duty whenever needed and had her bed placed in the hallway so that she could always be on call. Such mutual regard could not be dispensed with in a moment; one could not evade the sense of responsibility by merely saying "Here is your number one chit" (a good reference), "here is a cumshaw" (a sort of golden bowler) and, having done these things, depart airily and with a free conscience, remarking as a farewell "I hope you find a number one pidgin" (an excellent job). This sense of mutual dependency paid dividends later, for Li and Ah Ching did not desert their employer in time of adversity; a shortage of money to pay their wages did not result in their seeking another employer. It was very much this mutual regard and affection that bound her to Shanghai, tying her to the community when she could have moved elsewhere.

Nevertheless, not everyone who had enjoyed China remained. Some had other obligations which required them to go; individuals whose employment terminated or who were mere birds of passage moved on. Even those people whose whole working lives were spent in China felt the impulse to retire elsewhere; it was not that their roots were less strong or their affections less deeply held, it was necessity that prompted their decision. In this situation were Roderick and Muriel Mackenzie who had become Peggy Pemberton-Carter's best friends; they had sustained her emotionally during Florence Pemberton's long and difficult illness and when she had died they had taken their friend whole-heartedly into their circle. Together they had enjoyed three totally pleasant years.

In 1939 Roderick Mackenzie retired and he and his wife and two daughters crossed the Pacific to make their home in Canada. The city of Victoria, the provincial capital of British Columbia, had many others like themselves and they were able to find congenial society. However, the Mackenzies and Peggy Pemberton-Carter did not sever the ties of friendship; there were frequent letters, on the one side telling of the new life, on the other reports of the unchanged, or apparently so, existence in Shanghai. This correspondence was to be the origin of Peggy Pemberton-Carter's diary.

With the outbreak of war in 1939 between Germany and Great Britain, conditions for those in voluntary exile were largely unaltered. Nevertheless, the growing menace of the Japanese could not be entirely overlooked and "Extra-territoriality" might not be as potent as it formerly had been. Nobody wanted to believe that an era was at an end and Shanghai society continued to act as if it were rearranging the deck chairs on the *Titanic* despite the vessel's collision with the iceberg. The climax did finally come on 7th December 1941 when the forces of Emperor Hirohito attacked Pearl Harbor. The Japanese were now engaged in a massive military conflict with the United States and the British Empire. Shanghai was occupied and the Japanese armies took control. Extra-territoriality was no protection and Peggy Pemberton-Carter, like many others, was now an "Enemy subject."

In the military and naval sphere the Japanese were initially amazingly successful; the *Repulse* and the *Prince of Wales* were sunk, Hong Kong and Singapore — those supposed bastions of the empire — were captured, and the whole island world of the South Pacific was occupied. Australia seemed in imminent danger of invasion. In China itself Chiang Kai-shek and his soldiers were pushed far to the west. The future for the Allies seemed bleak.

When the Japanese assumed full control of Shanghai, they were quite polite to those who had once been protected by Extra-territoriality. At least initially their first Proclamation of December 1941 was full of honeyed phrases and promises. Nevertheless, it soon became apparent that the new rulers intended to be masters; the principal civic and business leaders were arrested and confined in Haiphong Road Gaol which was the headquarters of the dreaded Kampetei.[1] Peggy Pemberton-Carter's first direct introduction to what might occur was when her good friend, John Green, was among those rounded up. Years later she observed of that time, "One did not write anything down. Old letters, photographs, address books were destroyed. The fewer names, records, etc., the less frightening the prospect of possible 'questioning' by the Japanese Gendarmarie — the Kampetei, the local equivalent of Hitler's Gestapo."

In order to demonstrate the new order the Japanese authorities did everything possible to diminish the status formerly held by the "Enemy Subjects" with their prized Extra-territoriality. All of the Enemy Subjects when they were outside their homes were ordered to wear scarlet armbands with a number. Peggy Pemberton-Carter's number was B2268. This "distinctive decoration," as she calls it, was the local version of the Star of David worn by the Jews in Germany. She had said that while she had to queue for hours to

---

[1] *Kampetei* — The Japanese secret police.

collect her distinctive decoration at least the Japanese did not require payment for it. Apparently on occasion this planned humiliation misfired and the wearer of the distinctive decoration was offered a seat on the tramcar by a Chinese fellow passenger.

As each month went by more and more Enemy Subjects were arrested and it was clear that it was only a matter of time before they would all be imprisoned. By early 1943 a number of Civil Assembly Centres were being set up in several parts of Shanghai with Enemy Subjects from other parts of China being brought to the coastal city and interned. At the end of February Peggy Pemberton-Carter was finally ordered to report to the authorities and to take up residence in a prescribed camp. What happened thereafter is recorded in the journal.

Because she had corresponded regularly with the Mackenzies she decided to record her experiences in the camp in a style similar to that in which she had written previously. Her journal was to retain the tone of her earlier letters. She had started another account before her internment but had broken off when the Japanese began to make raids on homes and offices looking for what they deemed subversive material. She hoped, correctly as it turned out, that once she was interned any purely private diary that she kept would not be regarded as dangerous, nor would it be subject to prying on the part of the Kampetei because she would not be in a position to be actively hostile. Moreover, she was careful to be restrained in her commentary about the Japanese themselves and contented herself chiefly with reporting her own experiences, sentiments and feelings. Nevertheless, readers of the journal cannot fail to appreciate her antipathies and her attitudes.

It must be emphasized from the beginning that while interned she never suffered any form of physical brutality. However, she and her fellow internees experienced other aspects of imprisonment: the boredom of incarceration, the total lack of privacy, the relative indifference of the Japanese authorities to creature comforts, the sense of isolation from her real world, and long hours of physical labour. On the other hand, internment brought some compensations; the public and official humiliations came to an end, and there was a sense of community and a sharing with others in adversity. In addition, the Kampetei and the soldiers were on the outside, and there were fewer risks of sudden and possibly unexplained violence.

Internment is a unique sort of experience; it may best be described as being compelled to serve what is an indeterminate sentence. Peggy Pemberton-Carter remarked later that she and those with her would have found it easier if, like a gaol sentence, the terms and length of imprisonment were determined, for in that case one knows that at a certain point one will be released, but with internment one never knows when the end will come — today, tomorrow, this week, next week, this month, next month, this year or next year. The consequence is that morale suffers and there is pervasively a sense of pessimism. Moreover, internment required considerable social adjustment; to live a completely public existence without the possibility of being alone was far from easy so small pleasures loomed large — the evening concerts on the gramophone, a flower in a vase, the companionship of a pet, the importance of mail and of food and the rare semi-ceremonial event. News of Allied victories or defeats had a very definite effect on camp morale. Officially the only information allowed was that which filtered through the Japanese censors, but there were illegal radios. In Peggy Pemberton-Carter's camp the "farmers" who looked after the cow had a short wave set hidden in a brick stove and they provided their fellow internees with information. If their activities had been discovered they would have been summarily executed. Apparently in this instance one of the ironies of the situation was that those not in the know frequently criticized the farmers for being too polite and friendly to the Japanese commandant to whom they made the occasional gift of fresh eggs and cream. The Japanese knew that an illegal radio probably did exist but they never discovered it and little realized that it was so near Commandant Hiyashi's house and in the keeping of the farmers.

Rules and regulations were often petty. For example, in an effort to curtail the possibility that the Enemy Subjects might be able to bribe the guards or buy extra supplies, an order was given that any foreign money still held was to be surrendered. The amounts generally were not large and security was tight enough to prevent any real infraction of the regulations. Peggy Pemberton-Carter decided she would defy the authorities and take a risk by retaining a small sum she had in American Express cheques. The latter she hid in a box of talcum powder and luckily the Japanese never made a thorough search. After the war ended, she cashed some of the cheques in San Francisco — they reeked of the smell of the powder; on apologizing to the teller for their condition she was treated with great consideration and almost regarded as a heroine. The Japanese frequently imposed group punishment if one inmate violated a rule.

It was all rather like the teacher and a naughty class. However, it must be noted that the Japanese did allow the Enemy Subjects to receive the occasional parcel and letter, while the Swiss Consul as protecting authority was able to ensure that Red Cross packages did eventually arrive to augment the strictly rationed supplies, and there was even the rare opportunity to communicate with the outside world.

In December 1943 the Enemy Subjects were permitted to broadcast Christmas greetings (by radio) to Australia and New Zealand only. Peggy Pemberton-Carter's turn came on 24th December and because she had no family in those countries she decided, on impulse, to send a message to a New Zealand friend named Stanley Davys with whom she had been out of touch since early in 1941. Her message was picked up by the U.S. Navy and re-transmitted to Washington, D.C. where Stanley Davys was now posted; he was a member of the commission[2] responsible for the allocation of iron and steel. The military authorities took a very serious view of the situation. They refused to believe that this message for Major Davys from an internment camp in China was harmless and were convinced that it must be in code, suspecting it had something to do with spying. Davys was ordered to report immediately to a senior military officer and to provide, if possible, a satisfactory explanation to clarify the matter. This was not a difficult task for Davys was able to tell his superior that he was an old friend of Peggy Pemberton-Carter and that she was his daughter's godmother. On learning the facts, his superiors were immediately disarmed and Davys was allowed to return to his job. Peggy Pemberton-Carter never knew of the jeopardy in which she had placed her friend by her casual decision and it was not until 1970 that he informed her of what had happened.

What little is said directly of the Japanese is very cautious. This was partly to protect herself and partly because she was realistic enough to recognize that "patriotism was not enough" and that one could not blindly hate all of the enemy. Indeed, her opinion of the commandant, Hiyashi, is quite a generous one, for she believed that on the whole he behaved very reasonably, considering his difficult position and his duties to his superiors. She very properly distrusted and feared the Kampetei and the ordinary soldiers and knew that

[2] Stanley Davys was selected to serve as a member of the Allied Commission set up to determine iron and coal priorities. He was chosen because of his previous experience with the Swedish based Husquvana Co.

if they had a free hand the Enemy Subjects would have been treated with real brutality.

She reserves her praise for her fellow internees who remained cheerful and resourceful in adversity. She has great admiration for the men, the Taipans[3] of yesteryear who had lived pampered lives and who were now virtual coolies but who accepted their lot and the conditions imposed on them without complaint. These men never grumbled, they shouldered many responsibilities and burdens and coped with everything astonishingly well. The world would not necessarily regard their deeds and accomplishments as heroic, but they made every effort to ensure that the women and children suffered as little as possible.

By the summer of 1945 it was clear that all of those in the camp were becoming more desperate, both mentally and physically; confinement and lack of proper food were taking their toll. The end came suddenly with the Japanese surrender, and, the war over, release was swift; a new life with decisions to be made and responsibilities to be assumed was about to begin. The old existence "before" could not be revived. The last few weeks in Shanghai are reported very briefly in the diary.

The first and major concern of Peggy Pemberton-Carter was to decide where she wanted to go. Britain itself did not attract her much; she was without ties to the country, having only lived there as a child and while at school, and she had no family with whom she wanted to renew contact. Moreover, reports of austerity did not make the prospect more appealing for, all too recently, she had experienced enough deprivation. The solution was found when she decided to join her friends, the Mackenzies, in Victoria, British Columbia. To get there she had to pretend they were her family — which in a sense they were — otherwise, as a British subject, she would automatically be repatriated to England.

She had little to collect from the past; her possessions were few, her furniture had been sold in 1942, and her servants were provided for. A young lawyer in Shanghai made things simpler, easing the way through the bureaucratic regulations, and she was allowed to board an American ship bound for San Francisco. After a short sojourn in the United States she travelled to Canada. Victoria was to be her home thereafter.

---

[3] *Taipan* — The number one boss of a clan, family or business. The term was applied generally to the leading businessmen of European origin.

Her story after so many adventures and vicissitudes was to have one more unexpected event. Nicholas Abkhazi, the friend she had made in Paris and kept in touch with over the years, had become a French citizen and therefore was called up in the general mobilization in 1939. He was captured near Bourges in 1940 during the retreat of the French army and after several weeks in a camp in France, he and countless others were loaded into cattle trucks and sent to Hanover where he remained as a prisoner of war for thirteen months. He was then forty years of age and the German authorities decided to repatriate all prisoners of that age and over to replace them with younger men to serve as slave labourers. He returned to live in Paris under the German occupation. Existence for the next few years was far from easy but he survived. Following the liberation and the end of the war, conditions were such that he was now able to leave France. Time and distance had not diminished his regard and affection for Peggy; responsibilities and demands of others which earlier had prevented their marriage were now removed. Peggy Pemberton-Carter and Nicholas Abkhazi were married in 1946.

Perhaps Charles Greville, the nineteenth-century diarist, should be allowed to have virtually the last word. In January 1838 he observed, "A journal to be good, true and interesting should be written without the slightest reference to publication, but without any fear of it. . . . The habit of recording is first of all likely to generate a desire to have something of interest to record . . . it will exercise the memory and sharpen the understanding generally. . . ." Peggy Pemberton-Carter's diary fulfills these admonitions admirably; it demonstrates not only how one individual coped under circumstances vastly different from those of her previous existence, but also that people generally, even in adversity, do not lose their humour and their generosity, and that the human spirit can transcend its immediate environment and retain its innate values.

December 8th, 1941 to February 3rd, 1942

Shanghai

When the war struck us out here I was in the midst of reading Shirer's *Berlin Diary* and one of the first ideas when trying to devise some form of brain exercise was that I might try to compile some sort of week to week record of events. But after almost two months I find objections to this ambitious idea, some of them obvious, and the rest just temperamental. So if one is not to lose the power of coherently expressing one's thoughts or recounting one's doings in writing, which will surely happen after months or years without letterwriting, one must keep in practise by means of a personal notebook, or endless never-to-be-posted letter.

DECEMBER 8TH, 1941. The war started for me when I heard the furious sound of planes rushing over the house at 6:50 a.m. I thought sleepily "how angry they sound" and then a few minutes later Manfred Voigt rang up to tell me that Japan was at war with America and Great Britain. They had seen and heard the heavy firing on the river at 4 a.m., the sinking of the *Petrel* and the peaceful surrender of the *Wake*[4] as we learned later, but they had thought at the time that the guerillas[5] had crept up much nearer than usual. Tibbie Voigt and Manfred Voigt told me to come right away to them if I felt at all nervous up in my "lighthouse," like the dear good souls they are. John Green and Bob Lang were the next, and then Margie with the added information which was contained in a proclamation (the planes were scattering these over the city) to the effect that though Japan was at war, civilian lives and

---

[4] H.M.S. *Petrel* and U.S.S. *Wake* were small British gunboats that served as patrol vessels on the Whangpoo River. They were to protect British commercial interests and the British community in and around Shanghai.

[5] The guerillas referred to here were the troops loyal to various war-lords. Sometimes they supported the government of Chang Kai-shek but more often were virtually brigands.

property, even of enemy nationality, would be respected, there was no cause for alarm, though it might be advisable to keep indoors for that day, though everything possible would be done to allow life to continue in as normal a way as possible. Healey achieved some dignity during the 8 o'clock broadcast, the last one to come over XMHA under the old regime. An endless day, feeling stunned by the unexpectedness of it though I suppose no one can believe that statement who was not living here at the time. I imagine every single person must have spent hours at the phone trying to get in touch with friends to exchange reassuring messages as to their safety — the dialing tone was almost unobtainable — half an hour or an hour's wait was nothing. Funny how instantly one lost that demoniacal impatience over delay. David McLorn and Olive McLorn were all right, though for that day barricaded from the Concession.[6] I spent until the evening tearing up all my personal letters — some of them rather precious, but now that they have gone, it doesn't matter — liberation from something else — diaries, etc. At that time one did not know whether one would be allowed to stay in one's home, so it seemed a good idea to clear out every possible non-essential. Bob Lang came round after supper to see if I was all right, armed with some pie — a gesture so like him. We talked of yesterday's heavenly walk, with its perfect weather, good movie-taking, and the unspoken something that had suggested it was an end of an era, if only one of motoring, due to discontinuance of one's gasoline ration. Also during the talk, the idea of the pig farm came to birth, and re-planning the garden so as to at least double the vegetable production. I have not yet been able to steel my heart to digging up the lawn, hope the lengthening of the existing vegetable beds, and sacrifice of flowers and small grass patches will do!

DECEMBER 11TH. The bank opened for two hours business limited to one's being allowed to withdraw $500. Stood for 1½ hours in the queue, but it was no hardship, nice and sunny, immense friendliness and community of spirit from everybody, but why does it need a catastrophe to produce a condition which ought to be as natural to humanity as breathing? My wicked sense of irony had a few chuckles at seeing several people patiently standing who even last week would have sooner expected to drop dead than to be found queueing, and now they are not only carless, but jobless and well

6 The French Concession was territory administered directly by the French authorities unlike the International Settlement which was under joint authority.

on the way to being dollar-less. Made friends with a nice man, name unknown and shall probably never see him again, lost him in the wild surge up the bank steps, though he did his best to help me to keep upright. Next a cold two hours queue to deliver the registration forms and photos at the Gendarmerie in Hamilton House. The courtesy and extreme helpfulness of the Japanese is very striking. It has not yet failed in dealing with civilians. We had to declare all immovable property and movables over $10,000; furs, jewellery, bank balances, radios and cameras, guns and motors.

DECEMBER 12TH.   Queued again at the bank for the second withdrawal of $500. Alec Forbes a few ahead of me, and afterwards we walked home together — felt we were saving our bus fares, probably wore out more in shoe leather. To what has the war reduced him! Aside from losing his job, the same handkerchief for two days, and shirt for four. He looks badly, taking it very hard. Said he couldn't swallow his food, but persuaded him to eat roast mutton with me. Birthday supper at Mac and Olive's; Bob Lang escorted me there, bearing our own knives and forks. Strain and all notwithstanding, it was a warm and rather memorable evening. Bob played the fool magnificently, reading out the most succulent recipes from the *Boston Cook Book*, with true Hungarian drama and fervour. We all tried to convince ourselves that the report of the sinking of the *Prince of Wales* and *Repulse*[7] wasn't true — but I'm afraid it is. I suppose the politicians at home versus the navy, the old story.

DECEMBER 13TH.   Left home at 7:30 a.m. with B. for the third bank queue. Bitterly cold, but there was plenty to look at during the two hours wait, army and navy lorries, staff cars, tanks drawn up opposite the bank, and great activity at the Club, which is being taken over today. John Green being very philosophical about being dispossessed after thirty years residence there, but all the same it is a great wrench to him. He moved to the Palace Hotel[8] so I was able

---

[7] H.M.S. *Repulse* and H.M.S. *Prince of Wales* were two British battleships sunk by the Japanese off the coast of Malaya on 10th December 1941. The loss of these capital ships as a result of enemy action was a severe blow to allied morale. One of the many reasons given for the sinking was that the two ships lacked proper aerial support.

[8] The Palace Hotel which had been designed by the author's father earlier in the century was a very popular meeting place for Europeans who often gathered to have coffee and to watch the public passing by on Nanking Road.

to get his pipe over to him, as some mute sign of sympathy, poor lamb. A phone call from Olive McLorn and the promise of a priceless birthday present if I'd bring over the car — to have my tank filled up! Bless them. The poor girl broke down utterly, so I suppose I can take that as the answer to the question I'd asked myself so often. Don't know that it makes it any easier though. But I admired her spirit when he got back, tired and harassed.

DECEMBER 15TH. Queued at the bank again, but in vain. So returned home to get my photos and then back to the Astor House[9] to queue up for my request for special pass — 3½ hours. Extreme courtesy from the officials, and asked to come back the next day to receive the pass. When I got home Mac and Olive dropped in, so had a scratch meal, neither tea nor supper, by the light of a candle — 70% light restriction being announced, with penalties of 25 times the amount for any excess consumption.

Really life these days is divided between queuing, and then rushing home to bed in order to get warmed and rested and ready for the next queue. I'm still amongst the fortunate ones with heating and hot water, hence the innovation of Bob Lang coming over for baths. I must say one's sense of appreciation is sharpened to the most acute degree, and we are certainly all liberated from taking things just for granted. It is quite amazing how much one's interest is turned towards food and warmth. It doesn't take much or long for one to shed the finer intricacies of thought or imagination. On the other hand there is a great sense of comradeship with everyone, and a natural friendliness which I have never experienced before, excepting with one's very dearest. The absence of irritation or impatience at long and cold waits is something that makes me smile; I used to be amongst the world's worst waiters. Rigid if comic economies are the order of the day, as it would appear that the sole cause for anxiety at present is what will happen when one's bank balance is exhausted — it is all very well to be allowed to withdraw up to $2,000 monthly, *mais après?* Many families are doubling up, others taking one or more lodgers. Margie has taken in two Dutch couples, and they are running a "collective" household. My place doesn't strike me as suited to a lodger, and when I apply all brakes, feel that I can run it for very little, and today we hear that a rent moratorium has been proclaimed until March 31st,

---

[9] Astor House Hotel was taken over by the Japanese as their headquarters. It was situated in the Japanese Concession and their Consulate was close by.

and by then perhaps providence will have done something about the idle funds at Hansons.[10] I have descended to selling vegetables to my trusting friends — Li takes this badly and goes round with an air of "To think that I should live to see this decline in the family's fortunes," but on the other hand, he rather enjoys, and certainly co-operates in the new economy campaign. I believe he is living for the day when there is no more hot water and we have to heat it in tins over a chattie, *à la* Peitaiho.[11] He and Ah Ching are two more of my bits of good fortune, and though they know that wages may have to be cut, etc., are devoted and untiring as ever. Many people are having violent domestic trouble, even with old and trusted retainers. But to revert to the greengrocery department, during nine months of the year I ought to easily clear Ah Yue's wages and running expenses of the garden, so that it ceases to be a luxury. Further, Bob Lang and I have decided to go into the pig business, half and half. I think some money might be made, provided there are no restrictions when the time comes, about getting them over the line, but the young ones we propose getting won't produce until next autumn, so there is time for much to happen before then. At any rate they will provide food, and a strenuous, healthy occupation. I have gone into this question of occupation, now that all one's pre-war activities have been put an end to. At first I thought of some intensive study — Russian, or Chinese, or something to justify one's enforced leisure — one has so often said "I'd do so and so if only I'd the time," but now that that time has been thrust upon one, I find an impelling need for something physically strenuous, not mentally strenuous, nor emotionally exhausting. I suppose it is on the latter point that Bob Lang fits in so well with this phase of my life, we both know the limitations on both our sides, but he fills up many of the superficial chinks of my loneliness — very many of them, and I give him a kind of companionship he has never had before. I admire his resourcefulness, he has either lost (or thrown away, I'm not sure which) almost everything in life — wife, family, money, even health, his depressions are the most awful the world has ever seen — he isn't Hungarian for nothing! But still he emerges from them with some new

10 Hansons were the Shanghai law firm that looked after the author's affairs.

11 Peitaiho was a popular seaside resort much frequented by the European residents of Peking and Tienstin but also visited by people from other parts of China. It was very fashionable to holiday there living a "rustic" but comfortable existence.

idea, some *tour de force* of phantasy backed by a surprising shrewdness. He has taught me much, and I should miss him greatly in these days, but beyond that, our paths will always be miles apart.

DECEMBER 16TH. Only a week today, and it seems years. I think getting all the news from one source is one of the trials. My meanness is such that I will not buy a paper, and I rarely turn on the radio. What a lot of back reading we shall have to do one day to pick up the lost threads; and won't we be lovely audiences, only too ready to listen, though probably a little upset that others aren't showing as full an interest as they might over our little bits of news, what we ate when food ran short, what we did to replenish our battered wardrobes, etc! I hate to think of the anxiety of those on the other side of the water. Though I had fixed up with Alec Forbes to have his and my names added to the joint cable to Victoria, but silly Willie Smith of Jardines[12] forgot us.

Back to the Astor House to collect my special pass, a memorable queue, four hours, non-aryans (N.B. After several bus journeys, and what you sit amongst, feel I know why they are so partial to long neck-to-heel mackintoshes!) who cheated violently by jumping their places in the queue and drunken Sikhs. Upon one of the former — there were a couple of admirable ones — to be quite fair; I had the wicked satisfaction of implanting a well-directed kick when I came abreast and I have no doubt that this attitude of mind is what helps to produce wars, but having stood by that time for three hours in a suffocating atmosphere, my principles were neither high nor active. As queue companion I had charming young Dr. Laycock from St. John's;[13] at the turn of the stairs the situation got really ugly, the drunken and shouting Sikhs pushing, and the non-a's[14] swearing and shouting back, and then just as it hung in the balance whether the crush would turn to a stampede, a brave little Jewish woman called out "We mustn't do this, we must keep smiling," and the situation was saved. I shall always remember her. I was also much struck by the impassive yet courteous demeanour of the Japanese official who came to the first landing and just by standing there, quelled that milling crowd. It was the worst crowd experience I have been in.

[12] Jardine Matheson was one of the largest British trading companies in China. The Chinese called it EWO — "the princely hong" (business).

[13] St. John's University was an American university for Chinese students.

[14] "Non-a's" a term applied to Jewish refugees in Shanghai.

DECEMBER 23RD. Bob's compradore[15] today presented him with two small pigs as a Christmas present, so we took them out to Hungjao in the canvas picnic bag, poor little things they looked so scared. Argued with the bamboo man about the price of the enclosure — $155 is an awful slice out of the united capital. Then went over to Miss Fryer and picked out our two little sows and one boar, just six weeks old and looking so pink and babyish. She will keep them for us until the fence is built. So as to save rickshaw fares we walked all the way home and nearly died with the heat and a huge basket of vegetables. Bob Lang carrying the wretched thing and supposing it was worth the effort when I told him I proposed selling the contents for not a cent less than $4.

DECEMBER 24TH. Seeing that the pig farm has practically arrived it was no use wavering any longer over the bicycle question. The prices are hideous for an imported one as much as one used to pay for a small car. I went with Edna's husband and one of the Portuguese clerks from the Chase bank, and in the end got one for $680 — heavy as lead, but guaranteed for a year. Had the huge Peitaiho basket wired to the carrier at the back, so now am set up for the pig swill and green grocery trades. Mac and Olive, Alec and Bob came over for supper, a very contented evening, the men all looking the better for their meal. Clam soup, T-bone steaks, and one of Lady Stuart's plum puddings, finished it to the last crumb, and all said it was the best ever tasted, I expect real hunger had a good deal to do with it. By the way we all agreed as to our intense craving for sugar or any form of sweet food, I wonder if it is something needed to counteract half-unconscious anxiety and tension, though granted that we all take much more exercise.

DECEMBER 25TH. A strange Christmas day, one can hardly say happy, but a very thankful one. It was good to be with so many one cares for — I keep getting glimpses of what a brotherhood of man might be. It was also good to know that others are living in safety — or in as much safety as is possible nowadays — so I don't have to be worried about them, and yet if I were there I'd just be sick trying to imagine what was happening here. And then to make one laugh was the mixture of pre-war splendour and affluence with

15 A "compradore" did one of the negotiations between the Chinese and European businessmen. He was a "go-between" and frequently made a good deal of money from his activities. Every European company had its own compradore.

wartime economy and ingenuity, especially in the way of gifts, according to whether one had made one's purchases before or after the 8th. Plum puddings, candles, brandy, Heavenly bamboo fit in with the present scheme of things better than an ivory Kwan Yin,[16] perfume, gossamer handkerchiefs or stamps. Tea and supper at 490; all oppressed by the knowledge that Hong Kong can only hold out for a day or two at most. There'll be many anxious hearts here. Marie's Sydney Hill there, his steamer having been ordered to return south at the outbreak ... and they had already reached the muddy water near Woonsung, at the mouth of the Whampoo River — 20 miles from Shanghai. Vera's husband too, and her baby due in a fortnight.

DECEMBER 29TH.   The patient rice queues — truly the Chinese are a wonderful race with their endless docility — anywhere else in the world there'd be riots. A few agitators have tried to start them up, but so far without succeeding, and the patient souls stand there hour after hour, the lucky first couple of hundred with their numbers chalked on their shoulders, and the others trailing out endlessly along one block and down the side street and round the next corner, those at the end without the remotest chance of getting to the shop before the stock is exhausted. Sometimes they start standing the night before.

All private cars have been off the roads for just a week, and it has taken just that time for the Chinese population to forget anything they ever knew about traffic regulations. They amble down the middle of the roads, rickshaws go four abreast and little boys spin their tops in the middle of Avenue Foch and it is all rather enchanting; very like a holiday place. The tempo of life has slowed down to a delightful leisureliness, cycling one either passes or picks up both one's friends and people whom one has known for years but never actually met for months at a time, when we all rolled along in cars. And now going out even to tea so reminds me of winter outings when I was little, with your indoor shoes taken along to change into when you arrive, and the smell of hot oil and paint when one lights the bike lamp always brings back the warm sleepy excitement one was bathed in after a party. Talking of biking, I wonder why the wind is ALWAYS against one? And my knees are

16 Kwan Yin is the Chinese Goddess of Mercy. The author refers here to the many carved ivory statues which were popular as decorative objects in European houses.

always so weak and wombly, feel as though they are ready to bend backwards — don't think my joints are very well made judging by knees and that blasted little finger. Though I must admit that the latter isn't such a curse as it would be if the music were the soul's need it used to be; I hope that need comes back one day, but for the moment it has gone, deliberately buried along with all the rest which was so beautiful and so heartbreaking.

Grand total of vegetable sales for two weeks, $18.26. God help us, about as much as would have done for session at the hairdressers! The new era includes no more barber or manicures, no sweets, cigarettes, drinks, coffee or movies. And this plain living and high thinking seems to conduce to the healthiest possible appearance in almost everyone. Though the older men are looking a great deal older.

JANUARY 4TH, 1942. This year only made notable because of the installation of the three half-breed pigs. Duly christened Bill, Sonia, Tania and the Chinese ones, The Senior Concubine and The Misery. Also inherited Alec's radio. He is taking these days very badly; has developed a convulsive twitch around his mouth whenever he opens it to speak.

JANUARY 8TH. The pig farm is very engrossing, and the routine has been established. Bob and I go out with the swill and peelings on alternate days, excepting Saturdays and Sundays, when we go together. He rightly says that it would be worth at least 50 cents admission to watch us chopping the wood, drawing water from the creek — had to break the ice one morning — then crouching over the temporary primitive stove, eyes streaming from the smoke, feeding the fire until the mess is brewed. And then the pride and concern with which we lean over the fence commenting on the characteristics or increasing weight of each pig. The sense of property, I suppose, plus all the effort they involve. Feel pig gazing to be the only link of sympathy with my much hated Stanley Baldwin.[17] If ever we rear these successfully, and if we ever make a cent out of them shall write a treatise entitled "Pig raising under Difficulties." There will be one chapter devoted to the kind and quantity of clothes necessary to wear in order to keep warm and yet be able to cycle

---

[17] Stanley Baldwin, the British Prime Minister in the late 1930's, was associated in the minds of many with lack of British preparedness when war came in 1939. He was thought to be smug and complacent. A popular image of him was a countryman looking at his farm stock.

with enormous loads — 30 lbs at least. On the bitterest mornings I am clothed as follows (like a Chinese baby, if I fell down I'd never be able to pick myself up unaided!) woollen vest, stays, bra, woollen pants, silk ditto, old silk stockings, and another pair, thick hand-knitted woollen blouse, two sweaters, suede waistcoat, cardigan, gent's flannel trousers, jacket, scarf, fur gloves, these a pathetic reminder of past affluence, and don't in the least go with the rat catching effect of the rest of the regalia, and over all a mackintosh. Gone are the days of New York hats, suede shoes, neat suits and furs! Li and Ah Ching are towers of strength in this new venture when it comes to collecting scraps. Ah Ching has suborned the cooks at the T.B. hospital, and for $10 a month they are happy to swindle the official swill collector on my behalf. We get all from this building, and Li has a friend a cook at a boarding house who supplies us with a bag daily of vegetable peelings. So there will only need a little bran and bean cake to supplement this diet and sweeten Ah Yue's path. I believe that cumshaws, bran, etc. will work out at around 25 cts per pig per day. And the occupation is a godsend in these times, keeps one in the open with an illusion of freedom, and sends one home with a huge appetite (a drawback nowadays) and finally to bed and sound sleep.

Li announced today that he would like a holiday, so I asked him what he was going to do, he answered that he thought he'd like to walk out to see the pigs, and then walk on to see a friend who would give "us" some potatoes. Both objects accomplished, and I was presented with 20 lbs of potatoes with the injunction that I give 10 lbs of them to Tibbie and Manfred Voigt because I go there so often to eat.

JANUARY 10TH. Bitterly cold, with a fall of snow. John rang up, said he was wrapped in a jaeger dressing gown, and that he had developed such a fine sensitive sense of touch that now he could tell, just by laying his hand on the radiator whether the heating was on or off, but that if there was any argument between his cronies they just rang up the management to make sure. Pigs thriving, and getting tame in spite of my firm resolve not to cultivate them. It seems such black-hearted villainy to pet them and then lead them to the butcher. But the little wretches love having their heads and tummies scratched, and I am flattered that they know me, but won't go near Bob. A pleasant note of irony that I now have the scraps from the Nazi household behind me. And the Russians below me sent up (a) a bowl of turkey dripping that did not go to the pigs; it was the nearest approach to turkey that I have managed this year, and there wasn't a scrap of butter, lard or margarine to be had in the shops; (b) another bowl of soup which they had made too salty; I found that hot water soon cured that fault!!

JANUARY 15TH. Sonia with a cold in her tummy — truly why have infants when one can have pigs to worry over. Wrapped her up in straw (N.B. Where does the straw bedding go to. Pigs surely don't eat their beds. I pointed this out to Ah Yue who did not appreciate the irony.) and gave her hot rice gruel and hope for the best. Blessed the hospital and Chinese household for the rice — long may it continue, though I think it is immoral that they should throw out enough rice and fish daily as would feed a couple of the poor dying wretches lying around the streets. They never seem to worry about their own poor.

Olive McLorn's *bon mot*, that my legs in their hand knitted socks so reminded her of grand piano legs. And she is perfectly right. A charming letter from Huizenga[18] over my inability to pay for Ah Ching's weekly deflations — real Christianity, and something I shall not forget when the war is over and money is again available. The banks are to be liquidated, and it appears that half one's local dollar balance is to be frozen for the time being which doesn't improve the financial situation though I am still one of the more affluent ones with still $4000 to my name. I must devise means, for I already know of three or four who already have not enough to eat.

JANUARY 20TH. Richard Lang went out with the pig food, and found the barricades shut; Inspector Sharrock had been assassinated.[19] However by the afternoon they were opened again, and normal traffic resumed. Must lay in a stock of bran and bean against the emergency of not being able to get out to Hungjao. Bicycle convoys have been instituted, to combat the epidemic of being hit on the head and your bike removed from between your legs, which has broken out along Hungjao road. Most men ride along armed with knuckle dusters and lead coshs, but I am too involved with keeping an even keel under my loads, and anyhow

---

18 Dr. Huizenga was an American missionary doctor who ran a small hospital for Chinese patients. The hospital was near the author's residence in Shanghai.

19 Inspector Sharrock's death was the first real sign of overt disorder and a sign of things to come.

I am as always a firm believer in non-resistance when it comes to robbers, but the convoy system should work out well and be good fun also. The final refinement *à propos* of pig food . . . as well as simplifying the eternal transport question, has been provided by my mental brilliance . . . we now mince the peelings. The pigs like it so, it saves precious firewood, and thirty lbs can be pressed down into one pail, and Bob Lang and Richard Lang are willing to do the mincing. B. Lang here for his bath while I was out and indulged in one of his flights of phantasy with the eau-de-cologne — truly the man is an irresistible mixture of poet and child — all the past memories and reactions of a hurt child covering it up with a would-be boastful defiance. Perhaps I am feeling indulgent this evening but in these days of what seems to be perpetual cold, petty economies and unglamorous clothes it is nice when one has succumbed to the extravagance of a fire, and the lure of silk next to the skin, to be phoned up and told "You looked lovely" — even if . . . oh blast it all!

FEBRUARY 3RD.   The cycle bandits will go out of business for a time, as three of their number have been caught redhanded — two of them laid out by a Briton and a German, and handed over to the Japanese who promptly cut off their heads — so that is that.

Did accounts and things, and find that my actual living costs (no rent) for last month, food, light, gas, telephone came to $250 — bless the economy campaign. But oh Lord, the wages and rice allowance — $320. Vegetable sales, $47 and then Ah Yue goes out to the country with his wages and to buy bran and gets robbed of $75! It is perfectly genuine. I'm certain: he'd pinch a few pounds of bran, and as many vegetables, but not money — and his grief couldn't have been put on — it was too convincing without being dramatic.

FEBRUARY 10TH.   I can't write of the past week. Tragedy came very near the Lang family. Bob's anguished phone call to me is something I'll not soon forget. Where the original fault lies doesn't matter when any human being is so betrayed by another as to be driven to the verge of suicide.

FEBRUARY 17TH.   Singapore has gone;[20] hard to accept that fact, though C. prophesied its fall, and more besides, weeks ago. We are

[20] Singapore was captured on 15th February 1942; on that day General Percival officially surrendered to the Japanese army.

32

all just steeped in gloom over the news. Are we just born muddlers, and were we bluffing when we spoke of it as an impregnable island fortress?? In any case we have no Bataan peninsular to retire to, so, Java, Sumatra and Australia is the line of march, one supposes. The Japanese are understandably tremendously elated at their victory, and huge victory parades here and all over Japan are planned, but they still behaved with the same politeness and correctness which have marked all one's contact with them since the taking over of this place.

Private doings also off-schedule today. Bob Lang took out the pig chow, and I thought I'd try out the groggy leg with some walking, so went as far as the railway line, with the idea of meeting him on the way home to help with the buckets. Was told in broken English that my existing pass wouldn't do for Hungjao, must go to the Gendarmerie for another giving confirmation of owning the garden. So after tiffin set off down town, cold and dreary; found the Gendarmerie knew nothing about the new idea, but really they were more than polite and helpful, instead of sending me off to other and sundry Gendarmeries to find out for myself, which they might well have done, I being a good enemy subject, they settled down to telephoning which took something over two hours before they tracked down the necessary information. Didn't ask me to sit for a long time, and I wouldn't without being asked, but in the end even that courtesy was accorded. Finally, short of the simple solution of just letting one cross the line, they offered every other imaginable suggestion and compromise — rather typical. But I gathered that Ah Yue would be able to come in, and that after this particular spasm of barricading (Nanking Rd. also barred) — in other words when the terrorists are caught — we should be back to as we were. Got home feeling depressed, cold and tired, to find Li in a state of suspended drama and agitation. Four Japanese soldiers, to listen to him, armed to the teeth, had called and finding I was out, said they would return at the same time tomorrow. I couldn't think what they could want, but the thought of domiciliary visits is hardly reassuring, it has on occasion been the prelude to being taken for "questioning" . . . B. dropped in for tea, and we both shed some of our depression after hot cupsful, laced with some of Mary Stuart's brandy. Room bitterly cold, sat with coats on and a hotwater bag. Bob promised to fly over to my assistance if needed tomorrow, and later Manfred and Tibbie announced that they would come over and spend the afternoon with me, and John would wait till five for my telephone, and if I didn't ring would get in touch himself. So I felt surrounded with trusted allies, bless them.

FEBRUARY 18TH. The private ruffles smoothed themselves out as they so often do. Spent an idle morning in bed, keeping warm and resting the leg. Bob Lang rang up a couple of times to ask for news. Manfred and Tibbie arrived at two o'clock, and we had tea with some of Li's patent boiled bread, at 4:15 the visitors arrived — not so mightily armed as Li's imagination had depicted — and accompanied by a Russian plain clothes man attached to the French police. And all they wanted was to get me to sign a paper and in exchange to give me a sticker saying that they had requisitioned the car. A funny end for that faithful vehicle, but in these days of no gasoline and shortage of money, I'll be glad to save the $30 a month that the garage costs me. Bob rang to say that he had seen them in the neighbourhood, so I was able to tell him that the visit was over, all as courteous as one could wish. John rang to be reassured that all was well, and Manfred and Tibbie went home with quiet minds also. It only needs to be added that Ah Yue got in this morning without the least trouble and took out the chow. Gave him the money for the bran, and he showed me the patent patch on his pants where he proposes to secrete the money so as to outwit any possible robbers; also going with two friends and bringing back the stuff on a wheelbarrow. Hope it'll be alright this time — that $75 breaks my heart as well as the exchequer.

FEBRUARY 19TH. So Singapore has already been re-christened "Shonan," The Star of the East. The German community here has today presented its congratulations along with a million cigarettes. And there have been processions of decorated tramcars parading before an entirely apathetic Chinese public. Fireworks on the Race Course tonight, don't know how much enthusiasm they have aroused.

A high tea party here as a revolt against the petty economies. Tibbie and Manfred, Geary, Gimson and the Nashes, such fun. We four cyclists had originally planned to ride out to visit the pigs just for a treat! But weather and my wretched strained tendon stopped that and so they all walked over, and what appetites we all had. Li reported with joy that we had consumed seventeen eggs, one lb of bacon and one lb of corned pork. So he feels that the family face has been re-established after these weeks of darkness. Tried to play to them afterwards, but the finger is poorly, and the inspiration not

34

very noticeable. It is degrading to have to write that much of our conversation turned on food — it always does in these days. My contribution being that I can get an excellent supper dish for 50 cts — Chinese noodles and a few shrimps and an aristocratic clam chowder for 70 cts. Money is the other engrossing topic outside of endless speculations as to REAL war news. I have a feeling that "Junior's" [the typewriter] days are numbered — it is only logical if he can pay for the bike now that there are no letters to be written and surely these immortal remarks can just as well be set down in ink with a pen. I also believe that Li will shortly be visiting "me uncle" on my behalf — and I am lucky to have some legally hockable things which can bring in a little wherewithall. My very dear Mary Stuart has scoured out her drawers and cupboards and all that Perky can find are two leaky hot water bottles and one collapsible rubber bed pan and one yard of rubber piping and so a visit to Peking Road seems indicated, and one hears that good prices are being paid for even damaged rubber.

Susie is a very superior little dog these days, she has learned to canter alongside the bike on quiet roads and better still, to ride in the basket behind on the few occasions when it isn't loaded to the plimsoll line and isn't she superior in her attitude to the more unfortunate little dogs who have to walk. She thinks her motoring days have returned. And I don't mind being her chauffeur, for one thing if I am cycling after dark, no robber would come near me, because she keeps up a perpetual growl at any and all moving shadows. A story sworn to by Lady Maze, that two foreigners were stripped to their underwear on Avenue Pétain at 7 : 30 a.m.

MARCH. I wonder what we used to talk about before food and finances were the all-absorbing topics. My finances for the moment definitely looking up, as Hanson's Supervisor has been extraordinarily helpful, and has allowed all back rent to be paid up to the end of this month, and taxes ditto, and then $2000 for living expenses. The like of which has not been heard before. I found him a very charming man, in spite of our having no language in common.

The Angels with Dirty Faces come here twice a week for baths, and as much food as they can contain, to try and supplement the rather convict-like fare of the American Relief; no doubt it will improve later, but at the moment it is rather grim, and Bob gets thinner and yellower every time I see him. I believe he is in constant pain too, poor soul. And the *ménage* is always on the brink of an explosion, thanks to their conflicting temperaments, and the convention in which Richard has undoubtedly been brought up, i.e., all the family misfortunes are your father's fault. And I'm sure that this acts as a crust on top of the old affection he used to feel and show to his father as a little boy. If only they didn't have to live together I am sure they would be good friends. To me Richard is a dear, the first time I have ever been able to get on in any way with the young but I could lay him across my knee for his behaviour to his father.

Last week Bob provided us with enough drama and to spare. I think it was the 16th, he phoned me, and I could hear his teeth chattering, and he said he wasn't feeling well; so I went over and found him huddled in his overcoat, and complaining of frightful pains. He thought it might be gas inside, so in cheerful ignorance I applied hot water bottles, and made him drink hot tea and though he was a lamb and said it felt better I was getting frightfully bothered, wondering how to persuade him to have a doctor, or how to get Richard to persuade him, when as though out of the blue (though we afterwards learned that he had been anxious about him after meeting him in the morning) Dr. Dunlap, a surgeon, dropped in, said he was just passing; found Bob had a temperature, got hold of Paddy Ranson, who diagnosed appendicitis, and decreed an operation within an hour. Richard Lang very shocked and "little boyish," Bob Lang at his very finest. In emergencies there is always a dignity about him, and his speech gets a biblical turn to it. For the first time I realized what an appalling blank, if he didn't come out of the operation and he, sensing something of what I had just realized, took my hand, and said "But you know, I should be so glad to go that way." He achieved real grandeur then. And when I turned to pack his bag, I realized for the hundredth time that I have never met anyone who carried actual lack of things, through sheer need of the money to buy them or replace them with such a grand air as he does. I suppose I am the only one who knows of the minute margin of cash, even no margin now that the war has stopped all silk trade, and yet never by any stretch of thought would I call him poor. The ambulance arrived almost at once, and Richard and I made the joke that we were not going to miss the chance of riding in a motor, so we went along to the hospital with him. We were asked if we would like to wait until it was over, and I thought it was a good idea, partly because Richard Lang looked awful, like a tiny boy for all his six feet two inches, and partly because I knew that this was the first time that the possibility of death had been brought close to him, and he might as well have it impressed as firmly upon his mind as possible. It was easy enough, as it never will be again, to talk about his father and his fine qualities to him, and Richard was really rather fine in his admissions, when one remembers how difficult it is for the young to uncover their feelings or to make apology. I deliberately gave him a shock by suggesting that he open the door of the room we were waiting in, because I knew that the trolley would pass by, taking Bob back to bed. It did, and Bob didn't look a pretty sight, though I was thankful to recognize that the flush and snorting breathing weren't signs of death, but Richard didn't know that, and he had his bad moments. Paddy Ranson gave a good report, and this time it really had been a matter of hours between life and death, a beastly angry appendix.

He made a splendid recovery, in spite of something being left inside and having to be fished out at a second operation to our rage, and in ten days I was able to arrive one morning with his clothes to escort him home. It wasn't a very happy homecoming all the same, and really Richard was maddening. I'd made the most of my talk with him to Bob, and promised him that new days were surely lying ahead of them, though he musn't be disappointed if the old lapses recurred but I never dreamt that the wretched boy wouldn't put in an appearance the whole day. Poor Bob, what with being weak and tired was almost in tears, and when Richard did turn up he tried to cover up his shock at seeing his father so shaken looking, by a bravado for which I could have whipped him for. Oh, damn the young for being so cruel.

A funny disjointed fortnight followed: Li cooked the meals at Bob's place, and I ate there with him, nursing him, etc., and keeping him comfortable. Really it was the only solution, and what a dear he was. I never thought a man could be so gentle and sweet when suffering so much discomfort. For the first time in my life I have found that gratitude can be touching and not merely irritating. The father and son barometer went up and down in an exhausting fashion, until at last the opportunity arrived for me to suggest, though I think Bob thinks he suggested it!!! that Richard would really be much happier living altogether at the School[21] with which

---

[21] This was the school for the children of American families resident in Shanghai. With the outbreak of war between Japan and the United States it had been closed. It had been re-opened to serve as housing for single people.

he agreed heartily, so that will solve that problem, and I am sure that the fondness which is underneath all the time will have some chance of displaying itself once they are removed from such close contact with one another. The Hungarian and New England temperaments do not mix gladly. One blessing about this appendix business, it has disposed forever of the so-called stomach ulcer. Paddy Ranson says once he is over this, he will feel better than he has done for years.

MAY. We entered the butchery trade on the 3rd with poor Bill; he made lovely pork, and I was a little consoled when Bob assured me that he was dead in two minutes and never uttered a sound while being killed — the awful squeals were whilst he was being caught. I waited next door until the dismemberment started, when Bob came for me looking a delicate green colour, for which I rather loved him, and drinking a cup of tea with quite unusual fervour. Bill cut up at 61 lbs dead weight, and we got him over the line in two baskets borne by Bob and Li and my bike basket, no duty to pay, though we virtuously trooped into the Tao Tai's[22] office—at least Bob went right inside, and Li and I stood at the door ready to declare our portions if necessary, however I believe that the Tao Tai and ourselves quite understood each other and the situation, and so we parted with smiles. Being the first sally into commerce I was very diffident about charging $7 a pound for the meat, and $10 for brawn, but the usual unsuspecting friends and acquaintances were only too eager to buy, and by next day not only was there no more Bill, but the next pig was already bespoken. My wicked humour bids me add that Olive was only interested in sausage meat, the only commodity that was non-existent!!!! So very typical. Grand total, $423, which goes some way towards reducing the investment.

The noise of the pig-killing, both literal and metaphorical, produced a few days later a Mr. Wu, rather a pleasant foreign style Chinese who is starting up a pig farm a few hundred yards from the garden. He was wishing to stock up with Yorkshires, so with pride we showed him our huge Kathleen, and with assumed nonchalance young Sonia, whilst assuring him that the only one for sale was Misery. After several days of negotiations he bought Sonia and Misery for $400 and $200. Tried hard for another $50 for Misery,

22 Tao Tai office was the headquarters of the senior Chinese official in a local administrative district.

but I think Sonia is a fair price judging by what Bill brought in as pork.

The next pig-killing, that of Conky, was delayed by Ah Yue, or rather our rage with him for skinning us good and plenty (though really I don't think as badly as we first thought) in the matter of the purchase of the two new pigs, Rotten and Worse which he vowed were 50 lbs each and for which we paid $270 — probably he only robbed us of 50 dollars seeing that he found a buyer the next day willing to pay $240 for them — so in the end we didn't sell, though an added reason was that Conky fell mysteriously ill, and we concluded that Ah Yue would look after her better if we helped to save his face by keeping the little rats. Ah Yue's explanation of Conky's illness was illuminating. He said that she was so angry with us for not killing her on the specified day, with the butcher arriving and all, that she just got ill to spite us. I personally think the more scientific reason was some bacterial infection in the food during a few hot days. Anyway she was a terribly sick pig, and only saved by Wu and his kindness in giving her Sulfalanimide injections three times a day. They knocked her out each time — one day I especially remember, she looked to be dying, and old Bob was such a love, fixed up the fishing lines and insisted that we fish, to keep us busy as there was nothing to do to help the pig except leave her alone.

After three days she began to rally, and then hot milk and raw eggs administered in a feeding bottle I improvised out of the travelling enema had to be given three times a day; the poor little beast became so tame and took the food like a baby, that I felt ill at the thought that she was only being nursed in order to be butchered. Thank goodness there is a man in the partnership, or else I know it would develop into a Home for Aged and Orphan Pigs. A week later it was announced that she had eaten a "litty chow she self, and have go bathroom," so we concluded that she had recovered especially when she parted company with two huge worms. On the principle of not drawing the attention of the gods to the matter, Ah Yue ever after refused to mention her name in connection with the butcher. When the day was appointed he said he understood only he didn't savvy which pig! So we all understood each other beautifully. I was not even next door for this butchering — really felt awful about it, seeing that I had nursed the wretch, and she used to come running up to me for bread, would probably have let me catch her without a murmur to hand her over to the butcher. So I salved my conscience and sentimentality by allowing

Bob to superintend, and Yue only arrived to help cart home the pork. A hot and heavy job, especially as there was no rickshaw for Bob, except one ruffian who demanded about ten times the fare, which Bob haughtily refused to pay, so he and Ah Yue started to stagger along with about forty pounds between them, and I puffed along on the bike with nearly thirty. We had to pay the vast sum of C.R.B.[23] $6 for duty this time, just as well we were comparatively honest in declaring, because in backing my bike out of the office, I lost control and it tipped over, and legs and shoulders of pork littered the ground. However, once again we all understood each other beautifully and parted on the best of terms!

Conky had fattened up so beautifully in the month since she was ill, that she produced 64 lbs of beautiful pork, which we sold at $7.50 for legs and shoulders, $6.50 for everything else, and $8 for brawn. All C.R.B., shows how prices have gone up since Bill was killed. Grand total C.R.B. 440 dollars, equals fapi[24] $880. All disposed of amongst unfailing friends and acquaintances, with an unsatisfiable waiting list, all put down for the Next Pig. This will be one of Ah Yue's miracles — of which we have bought two more — they certainly do fatten up amazingly, double themselves in four weeks. No doubt the having been "kill inside so no can have puppies" (this is Li's masterly explanation of their condition) has something to do with this.

We find that Bill has left a legacy behind him, Tania being quite certainly in pig. Dempsey is touchingly devoted to her, licks her mouth clean after each meal, and then snaps at her if she attempts to get it dirty again. She isn't very amiable, but we pretend that is because she resents being made an honest woman of.

N.B. Kathleen has grown into a Mountain of Flesh. Must thin her down in order to make her more *comme il faut* for the beautiful boar Farren will lend us for to be her husband.

Dempsey now having come to an age when he must learn to live alone and like it, it proving a perpetual source of income to the neighbouring strong men, because each day he either climbs, jumps over or smashes his fence in order to return to his lovely Tania, and we have to pay to have him carried back.

[23] C.R.B. — The new currency issued by the China Reorganization Bank. It was to replace the inflated local currency. The Japanese ordered all foreigners to turn in their European or American currency as well and to accept the new exchange rates.

[24] Fapi — the old local dollar.

Waiting for Internment

S. W. JACKMAN

This initial section of the journal breaks off somewhat abruptly because the author began to feel increasingly uneasy. Not only were individuals arrested suddenly and without warning but the Japanese soldiers were increasingly inclined to attacks on the population merely to show their power. As an illustration of this state of unease, Peggy Pemberton-Carter recollected later one such time and her feelings. She observed "crossing the Hungjao railway line on the way out to the pigs. I was glad of Susie (the dog) and her moral support. As I approached the line there was quite a crowd of Chinese milling around and the Japanese guards beating individuals indiscriminantly with bamboos and pushing them — perhaps two dozen — into a tiny guardhouse that at a pinch might have held five. Next to the guardhouse an unfortunate peasant was strung up to a beam by a wire around his neck, his toes just touching the ground. I was too cowardly to turn round and pedal home as fast as possible, too frightened to intervene. I dismounted, showed my pass and prayed that the guard would be a dog-lover — he was so enchanted at Susie in the rear basket that he called out his fellow guard, and much patting and soothing noises followed and I was allowed through. In the late afternoon when I returned the guard-house was still packed, the peasant still standing — I was not proud of my non-solution of the moral problem." Obviously if things had been slightly different she would have found herself in real difficulties. Occasions like this were not isolated; people recognized that they were living in a hazardous world.

In the summer of 1942 life became more difficult, the currency was being devalued almost daily, there were more restrictions placed on the Enemy Subjects and permission was required to do more and more things. One was able to cope though, even if it were in a very limited way. However, one morning everything changed.

Peggy Pemberton-Carter's houseboy, Li, came to her much concerned and she remembers he said, "Missy, more better you sell everything, furniture, clothes, everything. In a few day Japanese come put tickets on everything, then everything belong to Japanese Emperor you no can sell anything." Li was as usual very well informed for a week later the Japanese issued just such an order. Li, however, had been busy. It was, she said, "Li's apotheosis, a mixture of grief, triumph and financial acumen. He took charge of everything, rounded up buyers from all over, bargained — he charged extra high prices to German and Swiss customers — cajoled and threatened. The result was that the beautiful penthouse and roof-garden were stripped of all their contents. All that remained after the mammoth sale was a mattress, pillows, a pair of sheets, one blanket, a few towels, one deck chair, one card table, one knife, one fork, one spoon and a few paperback books." For all of the contents of her penthouse she received the sum of two million dollars; her Chippendale dining table and chairs had sold for twenty thousand dollars — just enough to buy a new pair of shoes. However, the two million dollars were a useful augmentation to her now much diminished resources.

All that now was required was to await the visit of the Japanese. Since the receipts all indicated a sale in advance of the Proclamation there was satisfactory evidence that nothing had been done illegally. Within a few days the Japanese gendarmes arrived. Li had been instructed to usher them in and he did so with his usual aplomb, acting as if nothing were unusual. He offered them tea but with his own cups since his employer only had one, and then brought them to his mistress. The latter, trying to look elegant and relaxed in a deck chair, indiciated in a sophisticated and urbane fashion that she spoke neither Japanese nor Chinese but that her Head Boy would act as interpreter. Employer and employee had realized that this charade would be somewhat confusing but that the rules laid down by the authorities would not involve any major problems. As she tells it, the result was a conversation in mixed pidgin-English, Japanese and Chinese. "Head Gendarme: 'Rich house, no furniture carpets, curtains . . . why?' Li: 'My poor Missy, too many troubles, now not quite right, now quite crazy'. The Japanese had no alternative than to be satisfied with this curious explanation for Li had no further comment. Somewhat crestfallen and rather sheepishly the gendarmes departed." A victory of sorts was won by the Enemy Subject and her ally.

For the time being she continued to camp in her pleasant abode but late in the autumn things took a turn for the worse. Her landlord "The China Realty," an American firm, informed her that her lease would not be renewed. Her friend at the head office — he was an American and ostensibly still running the business but all of his actions were really controlled by a Japanese supervisor of "enemy business" — suggested that she should make some alternative arrangements because at the end of the year she could very well be evicted.

Being without furniture and possibly without a home, Peggy Pemberton-Carter decided that the best plan was to go and live with friends. A joint establishment was more practical and possibly more economical. She elected to live with the Stuarts whom she had known for a number of years. Lady Stuart was an elderly semi-invalid. Her son, Robert, was in his early forties and he and their "house guest" had many interests in common. There was also a Miss Perkins called familiarly "Perky," the nurse companion of Lady Stuart. Miss P. was one of those amazing persons who remained cheerful in spite of all adversity and having a nanny-like outlook on life, felt more than able to offer comments both grave and gay suitable to the moment. Lady Stuart, Robert and Peggy were, in a way, her charges and they were admonished and praised; the world was observed with opprobrium or disapproval. This traditional British attitude was good for the morale.

The Stuarts' household staff were less feudal than were Li and his daughter and by now they had all departed. When Peggy Pemberton-Carter joined her friend, Li assumed his functions in what was technically a larger establishment but with very much diminished resources. It was felt, however, that with some luck and reasonable management the household might be able to cope.

In addition, while all of the furniture bore the labels "The Property of H.I.M. the Japanese Emperor — not to be sold," for the time being it was still in place. Of course, at any moment the authorities could remove it should they take the whim into their heads to do so.

The house itself being commodious, all had space to enjoy their own private lives while sharing in many communal activities. They each had their own floor; Robert Stuart and his dog, Topsy, lived on the first floor; his mother and Miss P. and their dog, Judy, inhabited the second floor; and Peggy Pemberton-Carter and her Susie, the Scottie, the third. The only potential for internecine conflict was the meeting of the dogs on the stairs, all of whom loathed each other.

The united finances made it possible for the establishment to exist. The costs of maintaining the establishment were becoming prodigious owing to the rampant inflation. For the month of November 1942 it cost $6,000.00; coffee was $33.00 a pound, a dozen tins of milk were $46.50 and a ton of coal was $750.00. Two months later household costs were close to $7,000.00, electricity costing $1,560.90, a pound of bacon $25.00 and a hundred pounds of wood, $90.00. The only expenses that were not increasing were Li and Ah Ching's wages — they stayed constant but they were provided with food and housing in any case.

Rumours of civilian internment were heard on all sides but for the moment nothing happened. Robert Stuart and Peggy Pemberton-Carter, however, realized that their days of relative freedom would soon be terminated. Being young and potentially dangerous, they could expect to join many of their friends in the camps. Lady Stuart and Perky would probably be reprieved at least temporarily; ultimately they would probably be confined to a hospital or, as the diarist later said, "something"; "Or something" had become one's watchword, and everything was an improvisation to tide one over for a little longer.

The winter months were cheerless, however, the household struggled on. They had some food and a little heat — they warmed one room, that of Lady Stuart, to a hot 55°F. Everyone wore bundles of clothes; style and elegance were completely discarded for comfort. They managed to have some sort of Christmas celebration, but they recognized it was only a matter of time before there would be a breakup of the household.

Life became more complicated. Supplies were short everywhere. The pigs were a problem — there was not enough food and getting to them had become dangerous. The guards at the railway line were more truculent and more unco-operative; delays getting to and from Hungjao were normal. Waiting in the cold was a misery. The Japanese guards were less amenable, because they were supremely confident of final victory. It seemed as if the Greater East Asian Co-Prosperity Sphere[25] was becoming a reality and the imperial forces would triumph with complete Japanese domination of much of Asia. The general unease and uncertainty caused Peggy Pember-

[25] This was the official Japanese term for their expanded empire.

44

ton-Carter and Bob Lang, her partner, to come to a decision with respect to their piggery; supplies were running low, the prospect of loss by theft was more real, consequently Ah Yue, the gardener, was given the hut and the fencing and two piglets and the original proprietors retired.

Another difficulty revolved around the dogs. Food for them was scarce and their future was bleak. The question inevitably arose: should the dogs be put down? It was hard to part with Suzie but the grim decision was taken. Fortunately she was rescued at virtually the last moment. A Russian couple, the proprietors of a small fur shop who had seen Susie regularly and who had observed the cheerful little animal as she sat on the back of the bicycle in her basket barking death and defiance to all nearby Chinese, arrived and offered her a home. Susie went off cheerfully enough to be cared for. After Peggy Pemberton-Carter was interned she learned from Susie's new owners (who, incidentally, very kindly sent in some food), that the dog was well and happy. Another problem was resolved.

Susie was luckier than many of her kind. Indeed, the kind and generous Dr. Phillips, the German veterinarian, collapsed from strain and grief after putting down so many beloved pets — polo ponies, horses, dogs and cats. The fate of the racing greyhounds was to be more grim. When too old to race at the Canidrome, they were butchered and put into cold storage. Later they were delivered to the internment camps as a source of meat. Periodically one would be warned "Better not eat the stew today," and those in the know knew what that meant.

Finally the order came that more Enemy Subjects were to be interned. Peggy Pemberton-Carter recollects that there was almost a sense of relief when one's number was called, for the penumbra between freedom and liberty was demoralizing and depressing; now at least one would be free of certain forms of harrassment. Moreover, misery loves company and internment would provide companionship, albeit not always the sort desired.

The journal takes up anew when Peggy Pemberton-Carter begins to make the final preparations for her internment, with the story starting early in March 1943 and continuing until 1945.

45

March 4th, 1943 to September 12th, 1945

MARCH 4TH, 1943. This will probably be one of the last letters that I shall write to you before going into internment, or rather to the Civil Assembly Centre, to give the correct and official designation. You'll remember that the Japanese adore giving fancy names to things, and they have the naive belief that if you call a thing by some other name, the nature of the thing itself is thereby changed. So now according to them, we are not being interned, and we are forbidden to mention that unpleasant word in any of our letters.

I received a summons two days ago to appear at the Church House, as my name was upon the list of those who are leaving for Lunghua on the 17th of this month. Upon explaining the general sickliness of the household, I got an exemption until the assembly due to go in on April 5th.

During these last days of quasi-liberty, life has taken on a queer unreal complexion, as though one might be living at the bottom of the sea. One gropes around, looking for familiar faces, and then one suddenly remembers that they have already gone to camp. Habits and conditions that have grown irksome suddenly become precious in the face of totally new and unknown ones that confront one, with life in an internment camp about to become a *fait accompli.*

However, for each week of delay in our calling-up, the whole family yields thanks according to their natures or religious convictions. Mary Stuart, Robert and Perky to St. Joseph, as guardian of families. Myself to providence, with an aside, that though barrack-room life is my idea of hell, I'll not permit it to submerge me. On the contrary, if I can't pit myself against this adversary and beat it, I deserve to be wiped out. And the same idea applies to civilization, as we know it. Lastly, Li and Ah Ching express their thanks by burning joss sticks addressed to whom? — I really don't know, but they must be to some beneficent guardians of the Middle Air.

To look at my baggage, you would imagine that I am sister to the White Knight — there is even a rat trap, though I regret that there is no beehive. The hold-all (never more truly named) gracefully conceals the hardware and ironmongery departments. Saucepans, kettle, enamel plates and mug, knives forks and spoons, coffee pot, gardening tools, washboard, brush and dustpan, mop and ready-made shelves, a bucket and the bedroom utensil — evidently a corner in these chaste articles owing to sudden universal demand, child's size, $58.20.

There is also a sideline in drapery and haberdashery, footwear and drugs. A bolt of cotton material for those curtains, by means of which I hope to obtain an illusion of privacy . . . if I don't suffocate in the attempt. Sun hat, gum boots, tarpaulin, cheesecloth, sleeping mat, fan and fly swatter, towels, sheets, mosquito net. Then today I had further inspirations for comfort in camp . . . or is it for colonizing some remote and hitherto uninhabited region? . . . and I bought garden seeds, quinine and aspirin, wire, rope, nails and pliers, wooden clogs, still more soap, salami sausages, shoe laces, insect powder, pins, needles and cottons, and two tin openers. The last item brings us to the food, as you know, ever an important item with me! I don't in the least mind how my clothes (or rather lack of them) turn out, but I'd hate to be hungry. So every spare inch is being filled with tins of every kind, and the wardrobe consequently reduced to the bare minimum of slacks, shorts, shirts, raincoat, sweaters, heavy shoes and socks and fur jacket.

You mustn't imagine that all this has been thought out and assembled by my own unaided mental brilliance. A few messages have been smuggled out from the men who went to Pootung camp in January, and they gave one some idea of the things that would be most useful to take.

In what now seem far-off days, how often you and I used to debate upon what books we would take with us if we were to go into any kind of exile. I remember that we both agreed upon the Bible and Shakespeare, and for the third choice I decided for poetry, whilst you wanted biographies. For my forthcoming retirement I have packed three Penguin Anthologies of poetry, Shakespeare's *Tragedies*, a *Plain Man's Prayerbook*, Well's *Outline of History*, a Russian grammar, a shorthand primer and some crossword puzzles, which seems to be a selection that should do for most moods.

The thing that worries me most about this interning is the knowledge that you will be so distressed when you read or hear the news that all enemy nationals in the Far East are to be put into camps. I wish I could tell you not to be unhappy, because honestly, I don't mind. One has travelled so far in the months since December 8th, 1941, and it has been a comparatively painless, but very thorough, process of gradual stripping; first a leg and then a wing, so to speak. If one had been brought to the present state at a single blow, it would have been nearly unbearable, but by the here-a-little-there-a-little method it has merely borne out in practise what I have always felt to be true — the fact of wealth, property, home, possessions or even personal liberty being in themselves anything more than mere adjuncts (very enjoyable ones, needless to add) to personal contentment. You are sure to notice that I am not yet stoical enough to add "and a beloved person" to the list. Anyway, I have lost all of some items, and most of some of the others, and I am neither sadder nor happier as a result, but certainly freer, even though I am going to be imprisoned. So don't worry about me.

MARCH 30TH. Robert Stuart's *bon mot*, as applied to me. "Many are called but few are exempted" ceased to be valid on the 27th, when I became one of the chosen band leaving for Lunghua on April 5th.

In many ways it is a relief to be done with the uncertainties and the efforts at planning intelligently in the dark. Though of course, if the chance to stay out were offered, I'd certainly take it. We have played this particular game of blindfold chess for so long. On one's brave days it was a game that never grew dull, the adversary kept one guessing all the time, and the mental exercise was exhilarating, which, in the absence of almost all other mental stimulus, was all to the good. But on the bad days there were attacks of feeling that the whole game with its rules, moves in the dark and its stakes was just plain futility. And now one's helplessness in the face of Authority brings a measure of quiet acquiescence, and one rediscovers the restfulness of obedience.

So, after next week I shall become No: 20/61 for the duration. A change for the simpler and quicker after my many christian names and impressive hyphenated surname which always shed such an aura of "hoch wohlgeboren-ness" when we were in Germany together, but which are now extraordinarily tedious when it comes to marking all my camp gear and filling in the ten thousand different forms appertaining to internment.

APRIL 7TH. I left the house at 7:30 a.m. on the 5th, very nearly clad in the shorts that have caused so much heartburning as a result of the rumours that the Japanese would not allow women to wear these useful garments in camp. The reason for so nearly having to leave home pretending it was a summer's day, was an eleventh hour accident with a thermos flask, which nearly caused me to be drowned in a flood of scalding hot beeftea. But my devoted Li accomplished a miracle with hot water and an iron, so I was able to depart more decorously and suitably clad.

Little Ah Ching tried hard to be brave, and Li was quite admirable, getting over his tears at home, and so fulfilling his promise to me that he would behave like a man when we got to the Columbia Country Club.[26] I had pointed out to him that any exhibition of grief would only give greater satisfaction to the Japanese.

The family were just as one would have wished, and having heard that the Scottie is happy in her new home, I was able to set out quite light-heartedly, under Robert's guidance, feeling all the while that it was happening to someone else.

On the way to the Club, I saw a Union Jack for sale at the Thieves Market. It looked a pathetic emblem, lying in the mud and garbage on the pavement. How are the mighty fallen — temporarily!

Once at the Club, the missionary ladies who had been billeted there ever since the Japanese brought them down from their homes up north, were untiring in their efforts to make us feel at home and as comfortable as possible during what would undoubtedly be a long wait. The place was well heated, a luxury I haven't had for months, there were armchairs, and we fortified ourselves with endless cups of tea. I found many acquaintances, everyone was very cheerful, and nobody showed the least impatience. I guess we all felt that with probably years of internment lying ahead of us, what was a mere two and a half hour wait for the buses that were to take us out to Lunghua.

Eventually eight French buses rolled up, and just as I was embarking in one of them, Monsieur Marchand ran forward to say good-bye to me, and he added how sorry he was to have to be

26 The American Country Club. *The* Country Club was British.

escorting me to such a destination. As French representative he had to go with the Japanese Consular representative, to make it all seem nice and legal and tidy. So "Authority" went in cars ahead of our lumbering cavalcade, and we set off at 11 o'clock.

There were a few hand waves en route, and some non-armband wearers accompanied us on their bicycles. The Chinese just looked on stolidly.

We arrived at the Lunghua Middle School about 15 miles outside Shanghai, right out in the country near the historic old Pagoda, in half an hour. My first impression — "There probably are 480 *mow*[27] of land, but not a bush or a tree" — So visions of leisured hours under trees evaporated at once. The nearest approach to shady trees for purposes of solitary meditation being provided by two piles of devastated buildings and an acre of bricks.

The actual school buildings are fairly impressive at first sight, and the men have been marvellous beyond all words, accomplishing miracles of repair, cleaning, building and organizing, and hauling our beds and heavy baggage.

The fortnight-old inhabitants were up on the roofs and at all the windows, waving us in. One wit had produced a banner inscribed: WELCOME HOME.

I have been billeted in one of the wooden huts, B West. My first thought was "Barrack-room life with a vengeance" when I saw the long vista of beds (51 of them). Really the length of the hut appeared so terrific that I wondered how on earth I'd ever be able to walk the whole distance. The wooden huts East and West were designated for women without husbands. One can follow the intellectual struggle with the fine points of a foreign language. "A-a-ah — so desuka! Women alone-unattached, unattached-not tied, loose — THEREFORE: 'Loose Women' is the correct term." And *so* we were known.

The alternative of going to live in a room with eleven others was offered to me, but I declined it, for I am sure that there is more chance of solitude in amongst a large crowd than in a small one. Especially as my bed is right at the top end, a scorned spot because of endless openings and shuttings of the door to the washroom and toilet. This doesn't bother me, for once there has to be noise and crowds, a little more or less makes no odds. I find my old powers

[27] A mow is a local Chinese measurement of land, about one-sixth of an acre in area.

of concentration have not deserted me, this is being written to the accompanying noises of said door, and the chatter of 25 adults and 2 children. Myself seated in my canvas chair, feet on the tin trunk, and the washboard for a writing table.

The great advantage is an extra two feet of corner wall for hanging up purposes.

The windows are low, 28 to each side, and there are double shelves along the walls. A welcome surprise, this. We have three coal stoves burning brightly, the one cheering feature within sight. Doubly welcome for the weather is vile, bitterly cold and it rains all the time. But I must add that I have extracted a priceless blessing from all this rain — out go my bucket and saucepans to collect the precious stuff so as to elongate our meagre water rations.

We have electric light, which I hadn't expected. The lamp and switch are over my bed, for which I yield thanks, feeling that control over these probably prevents acrimonious arguments from developing!

In the washroom there are cement troughs round three walls, with cold running water, but so brackish that no soap will lather, however, even so it is an unexpected blessing. The toilet room opens out of the washroom, there are two small wash basins here with the same running water, and six flush toilets. To be accurate, only three of them flush, which is to say, they flush when they feel like it, but they are very temperamental, and to encourage them we have had to chalk up the legend: DO NOT PUSH UNLESS VERY NECESSARY.

The rations are quite good as regards quality and being served hot, but the quantity would leave a void in one's interior if it weren't for being able to supplement with one's private store, either of tinned food or the fresh food we brought in with us.

Today's official menu: Breakfast: Rice congee, 2 teaspoons of sugar, 4 ozs of brown bread and green tea to drink. Lunch: 2 herrings with curry sauce, potatoes in jackets, tea. Supper: meat stew, chinese cabbage, 4 ozs bread, tea.

As supplements I add soya bean milk powder to the congée, and either dripping or honey to the bread, and I still have some fresh fruit from the food I brought in.

Getting our meals is no simple process, we queue up out of doors in two double lines, when we reach the dining room building we each pick up a tray, if there are any left, and set our knife and fork and enamel plate upon it, then get ration card marked, receive our portions and pass along to the long benches and tables. There is a certain technique amongst those of us of the second sitting; we eat as slowly as possible, and sometimes the welcome cry is heard — "There are some second helpings." I suppose it is needless to add that we are always hungry, partly due to the country air and partly because we are endlessly occupied with our endless comic chores. After finishing our meal we go to the washing-up line, first stop at the swill can, next at the running cold water to rinse, and then we dip our things in a tub of boiling water and dry them with our own towels.

Today's best remark, uttered while we were standing in the rain and wind, and had been so doing for some ten minutes — "Now move up, so that you don't get the drips from the roof."

A VIGNETTE OF DORMITORY LIFE.   Myself standing with damp laundry wrapped around the stove pipe, trying to toast it, after two days of unsuccessful efforts to dry it by more usual methods.

The greatest problem is the water, but it has been very well tackled. Hot washing water is served at certain hours at Bubbling Well — the new name given to give us a homely feeling, to the brick stoves that the men have built near the creek. Here one may have as much hot water as one can carry, by paying for it in cold water which one gets out of the creek. The drinking water is boiled for us, comes from the Lucky Dip, presided over by the Lady Dippers. We meekly queue up with our thermos flasks, and pray that the fires are burning well so that we shan't have to wait more than half an hour in the everlasting wind and rain. For wet clothes here mean something quite different from wet clothes at home, where you can get them dried!

The Lucky Dip's early morning cry: "All kinds of water, wet water, dry water, lavender water, whiskey and water, hot water, clean water and dirty water."

The most comic feature is the complete lack of time. I'd had visions of long hours of reading, studying, or knitting, whereas there is no time for anything, even the smallest personal chore can only be accomplished after a dozen interruptions. For example, this wandering letter to you has been punctuated by (1) A wild rush outside to nail a strip of wood across my window which threatened to blow out in the near typhoon which is raging. (2) Another outing to replenish the coal bucket. (Piling on the coal is our greatest pleasure — we feel that we are getting some of our own back from

53

the Japanese.) (3) Drinking water queue. (4) Toilet patrol. (5) Arranging and watching the buckets out collecting rain water. (6) Supplementary meal with next door neighbours. (7) Dormitory patrol. Having been ordained a sub-monitor, there are Certain Responsibilities.

This is a typical day's routine: About 6:30 a.m. a stirring begins in the dormitory, and gradually the 49 of us get ourselves up and washed with the various dregs and drips of water we have managed to conserve from the previous day. Make beds, sweep and mop the area of floor around and under our own bed and half the passage way down the middle of the hut. Breakfast at 8:30. Then dormitory duties. This morning it was my turn to clean the toilets; extracted the inevitable cottonwool stuffed down the so-delicate drain, in spite of addresses upon the subject having been delivered by our monitor. Drinking and washing water queues. Half hour of Toilet Patrol, this latter is one of the few opportunities for solitude and meditation — the surroundings leave much to be desired, they are cold and unaesthetic, but at least there is quietness. Lunch is at 1:15, then I put in my two hours of camp work. Gardening is my choice — there'll be holidays on wet days, whereas peeling potatoes goes on for ever! Drinking water queue for one's afternoon ration. Supper at 6:15, and by 8:30 a certain weariness descends. Undressing and washing the same wearisome and uncomfortable processes as dressing. Lights out at 10:30. And I, the wretched sleeper at home, don't know much about anything until the next morning. Only vaguely hear snores and sighs and groans and the accompaniments to communal night life.

This afternoon quite a long Proclamation was posted up, from which the following is a delightful extract:

This Civil Assembly Centre being the best home for those who live in it, must be loved and cherished by them. All persons shall take care of their health, and live in harmony with one another. There shall be no disputing, quarreling, disturbing or other improper demeanours.

All of which are very proper sentiments, though I don't know what opportunities there'd be for the last item, unless it is amongst the bricks . . . Love Among the Ruins, up-to-date.

APRIL 9TH. This is the kind of mental gymnastic we indulge in. Tonight we ate the last of the chicken I'd brought in, so soup was the obvious solution for the bones. We raised enough water by begging for two dippers full, and my bucket was the logical receptacle to cook it in, though I had arranged to use it for clothes washing tomorrow. We bespoke the stove for simmering it after we had gone to bed, and then it will need another hour in the morning on the outdoor stove, (we don't light our hut ones until the evening), between the time the last breakfast sitting ends and the gardening duties start. Someone else will have to do my dormitory chores whilst I watch the pot. All our united ingenuity has failed to produce an onion, but short of that it will be wonderful soup.

Really life isn't too bad, there's not an anxiety, our duties are all prescribed, the food at present is adequate. And most important of all, one meets kindness and generosity on all sides. I wonder if these qualities will dwindle once deadly monotony gets us in its grip.

There are some odd facets to life, and one runs into the oddest characters — knowing all the time that one's own character is just as odd. The most notable discovery is that there really exist people who are not house broken. I'd read about it when some of London's slum children were evacuated to homes in the country, but I could never believe it, and certainly never expected to meet it.

And there is a famous family in the camp — gifted, artistic, dirty, lazy, liars and shirkers, unimaginably insolent, and yet at times charming beyond all words. There are enough of them to be a law unto themselves, so they sail along entirely oblivious of anyone else. It will be amusing to see, as time goes on, which wins — The Family Law or that of The Herd.

I believe I have met the world's champion grumbler. She has the kindest heart imaginable, but at the same time scatters such clouds of misery and complaints that everyone flies at sight of her or sound of her foghorn voice. She has developed a perfect "schwämerei" for me, and dumps herself at all hours upon my bed or camp chair, to the ill-concealed mirth of the whole dormitory and to my rage at thus being deprived of the sole corner I can call home — for then I have to resign myself to listening to the interminable flow of grumbling. "The trouble is I've no teapot, and nobody wants to swap one for my extra pair of pliers ... I've no bucket ... my washing water hour is too early. I should have thought that someone would have changed with me, and I can't get my drinking water in the afternoons because I always rest between 2 and 3 o'clock ... and I've no more peanut butter and I was such a dumb cluck that I never asked my friends to send me any — not that I've any friends outside. I can't eat the bread and I'll have to open my last tin of sausages, and the Billeting Officer says that all the friends on the list I gave him have made up their own parties of room mates, and I'm in with strangers, and the trouble is . . . I should have thought . . ." and so on, ad infinitum!

APRIL 17TH. ANOTHER VIGNETTE OF CAMP LIFE. The battle at the open air stove between voluble Russian women and equally dour Scottish ones. Victory went to the silent ones, but it was ridiculously funny to look on at them. All looking smoky and windblown and pinched with cold, each one stirring her own private witch's brew, excepting Scotland, who presided in arrogant silence over their Dutch Oven, seemingly oblivious of the running commentary from Harbin. . . . "Baking cakes is a luxury . . . even making puddings you can do without . . . I work in the dining room and do my washing and must cook for my husband and child who is sick . . . the best must be saved for the children . . . my pot has been on for two hours and it has not yet boiled . . ." And always the contrapuntal theme, "Baking cakes is a luxury, and making pudding you can do without."

It has been a cold dreary day, with gray skies that make the perfect background for the dazzling brilliance of the golden rape, and all the shades of green, from the palest one of the new wheat to the near black of the fir trees in the little burial ground just beyond our boundaries, and the soft violet green of the beans — just the right shade to go with their intoxicating perfume which blows over in great gusts on the damp wind. Beyond the green are the black curly-eaved roofs and gray white walls of the farms, and as I write, I can see just one Chinese woman walking along the path to her home, and she is wearing faded blue cotton, with a white cloth on her head. All things I've seen ten thousand times before, and all that prevents me from being amongst them are four strands of barbed wire, Enemy Authority, and worst of all, simply nowhere to go to, once one was on the far side of the wire.

It is a depressing thought that this hideous place with its huts, ruins, gaunt buildings, makeshift camp kitchens, hot water boilers, scraps of wood, broken glass, bits of wire and straw, mess, dust, mud, smells and dirt, with straggly grass trying gallantly to turn green for the Spring's sake, the general treeless ugliness, all this completed by the shabby humans with silly faces and bleating voices (self included) is the nearest approach to home that we, any of us, possess at this present time. All this outburst sounds like the indigestion which is actually gnawing at this Woman of Tralee —

56

do you remember our delightfully vulgar limerick? But moods change quickly here, and from this morning's nostalgia and depression to this evening's cheerfulness is a swift journey. The change was induced mainly by the arrival from Pootung of four men, fathers of girls in this dormitory, who have been transferred here. An interesting interchange of news and messages, the latter neatly concealed between the outer tin cover of their thermos flasks and the inner glass. So, another excuse for a party — we have one on the least provocation, each donating a tin. Tonight K. and E. are donating sausages and rusks, and myself peaches and coffee. This will give us all a sense of well-being, much needed as the official rations have deteriorated considerably during the past few days.

Needless to say, food is our sole delight; we think, dream and talk about it perpetually, and I have even noticed that cook books are the favourite form of literature with at least two inhabitants of this hut.

Another odd feature of camp mentality is the resurrection of 4th form schoolgirl humour — hardly dignifiable by that name, a primitive sense of fun is nearer the mark. For instance, if someone else's (not your own, note) bed leg crashes through the rotten flooring of the hut, it strikes us all as exquisitely funny, and we all collapse into helpless giggles. And when the Commandant does his official roll call (about once a week) we behave in a manner unbelievable in more or less sophisticated women of ages varying from 25 to 50, not counting the actual girls. We stand demurely, as ordered, each at the foot of our bed, and he walks swiftly down the aisle, murmuring "goodnight" to each of us, his bodyguard of two gendarmes standing at the door. (There are only 35 gendarmes as the sole sign of armed authority in the whole camp of 1,200 internees. The rest of the guarding is done in volunteer shifts by our own men, two hours at a stretch.) Then the moment the door closes behind the trio, an uproar of chatter and laughter breaks out. Once the wave broke just before the door closed, and there was a consternated look in the eye. Trying to be fair, I think Hiyashi is well-meaning, but my feeling is that I don't trust him in the least. And in my moments of fury, I'd love to have him recount the bitter experiences he has spoken of that occurred during his internment in London — at the Savoy Hotel.

Here are some lightening portraits — to make you laugh. This cold, wet, cheerless morning offered one gleam of metaphorical sunshine. Celia Mary Napier, wrapped in a brown frieze cloak, came smiling to my corner ... "Look, Spring is here ..." and showed her bunch of dandelions — and I really felt revived. There is K. our champion ironer, if you can call it ironing. She achieves miracles of smoothness upon our blouses, even pleated fronts undertaken, by a series of astounding evolutions around the stove pipe. She is a good-natured rascal, as fat as butter.

Then there is Babbie who, by some peculiarity of voice, underlines every second word, and infuses Drama into the most commonplace occurrence. She rejoices in cleaning shoes more than in anything else in the world, she polishes them with religious fervour and demands our unqualified admiration. At other times she appears to be permanently engaged in stewing a great pan full of dates, or else composing (out loud) anguished letters to her absent beloved.

We also have Irish Mary, with her head swathed in a black scarf, a long twisted underlip, looking like the perfect Irish tinkerwoman, even to the pot of black tea which stews all day on the hob of the stove. She has a dry, complaining sense of humour, a small dose of which is very droll. A strange combination of kind heart and bitter tongue, with a capacity for talking that I have never seen equalled. During the first five minutes I met her she skimmed over an incredible number and range of subjects. Every inch of ground was covered, from a simple and safe home method of procuring an abortion to how to boil rice successfully.

But the star occupants of this hut left before my arrival — translated to other spheres, to the relief of those left behind. However, they acquired such legendary fame that I feel as though I have shared sleeping quarters with them. I have seen the husband several times, darting about the compound in a terriffied manner, looking like a scared black rabbit, with an old beret smashed down on to his ears, several gold teeth, spectacles and dirt. I think Arabian Jewish. Mamma, and a girl of 6 and boy of 8 slept in one bed in this dormitory for two weeks, and during that time were never once observed to move off the bed. For the first few days they lived entirely upon raw eggs and cream puffs. When the latter gave out, the husband used to bring in their camp food, but during the nights cracking noises proclaimed the fact that Mama and family were still keeping up their strength with the raw eggs, the shells of which were strewn upon the floor. None of the three ever washed during their stay; they kept most of their garments on day and night, but any surplus garments were kept in or on the bed, and strange messes of food and oil were parked under the bed, alongside of Jeremiah

58

Esq., which was put to its legitimate employment in and on the bed by all three. One night there was such a splashing that Muriel Porter as monitor, conscientiously turned on her flashlight, thinking that the roof must be leaking — but it wasn't the roof leaking! Next morning the Health Officer agreed that they might be better in a room to themselves. Incidentally, Papa assumed the defensive attitude of always being engaged in prayer whenever called upon to try and persuade Mamma to lead a slightly less naturalistic mode of life. I have often watched his terrified efforts to squeeze in between two Russian viragos already in possession of the beforementioned communal stove, so that he might prepare a great pan of curry, apparently the only form of nourishment, apart from the eggs and cream puffs, that they ever partake of.

APRIL 23RD. Yesterday's highlight of ridiculousness was reached when one stove in our hut caught fire through a fall of soot, and our sole fire bucket was at that moment being used by the monitor, who was busily engaged in washing her feet. How our dour, woman-hating Fire Chief would have groaned, had he but known. Poor wretch, I think he is terrified of the female sex, and so tries to protect himself in an armour of ponderous bitterness, which reduces us all to helpless mirth, and himself to consequent inarticulate rage. In the end he never manages to convey a single concrete instruction of what we should do if fire broke out. The best he can manage is: "Rotten, ladies, just rotten. It'll have to be 100% better next time I come to drill you." And then he stalks away angrily. Anything we have learnt is thanks to his assistant, a Welshman full of charm, who has the art of making even a bucket chain interesting.

On the 19th a huge batch of newcomers arrived — some say the last lot we'll have, as our numbers are now up to 2,000. Our hut is full to bursting, with 53 inhabitants of all ages, classes, habits and nationalities and religions. A liberal education in the humanities! Apart from superficial irritations, I think it is wonderful how well we have all shaken down together. It would appear that the difficult minority are nearly always becoming assimilated by the more normal majority. So here we are, Belgians, Dutch, Russians, British, Dutch-Japanese, South African, genuine Portuguese and half castes, French and American, of all ages between 13 and 60.

Our new Belgian inmates looked very bewildered upon arrival, and the family, the Baron and Baronne Guillaume and daughter Jeanine, claimed long and interested scrutiny from us all. Madame erected a wonderful tent-cum-canopy over and around her bed even before she had unpacked a suitcase — as older inhabitants we feel she will loosen up shortly and dress and undress in a less complicated and exhausting series of evolutions than at present. Rations were particularly poor at that period, and we watched with watering mouths the Baron, Baronne and Baronnette sitting down to their brought in food, cold fowl — two helpings each — (we thought, "Make the most of it, and Oh Lord! don't let them suck the bones, they'll make soup." I nearly went up to them to say in my best French, "Allow me to throw away your scraps.") — then they had cheese and crisp bread, and apples, and, I suspect, *vin rouge*, decorously served in a thermos flask. And their table was covered with a gay checkered cloth, with napkins to match. How far we have fallen in under three weeks!

One notices the ferverish way in which newcomers wash themselves, their pots and their clothes — they start in on the latter the day after they come in. But after a week or so, a more reflective state of mind sets in on the subjects of Washing Water and Drinking Water; and the two dippers on alternate days of the former, and three pints daily of the latter are exploited to their fullest advantage. And one is cleanish, if exhausted by the mental and physical efforts expended on the subject.

Now that the hut is full to capacity, and changes unlikely, I have dug myself firmly into my corner, with every inch of space utilized. On the 18 inches of extra wall space I have because of the washroom door, I have put up two hooks for my clothes, a small shelf above, which holds books, and a curtain made from my kimono hangs from the shelf, which helps to keep the clothes slightly protected from the eternal dust. My corner window just permits of my chair being placed so that I can put my feet up on the window ledge. One small trunk and three suitcases and the bed occupy the remaining floor space. The bucket, "iron rations" of tinned food, oddments of wire, wood, glass, and other trifles which one picks up because they may come in handy some day — and the day always comes, all live under the bed, along with anything else that you simply can't bear to look at for another moment. So here ends my complex about always having the floor under the bed free of everything. The folding table, washboard and deckchair rest against the wall at the bed's head, and above them a shoe bag arrangement with compartments to hold toilet articles. On the lower shelf stand my two thermos flasks, two saucepans, frying pan, coffee pot, teapot, plates and mug, kettle and mirror. On a tiny extra shelf — also my own erection, (and our pride over any bit of handiwork or display of ingenuity is really pathetic) stand writing things, ink, soap and manicure case. Alas! my pale musician's hands are now objects to make one laugh or weep at, all sunburned and calloused from the gardening. And excepting after clothes washing, they are never really clean, and the nails are far too short to do more than make a pass at with the cleaner.

The topmost shelf holds gumboots, small medicine chest, dustpan and brush, scrubbing brush, tool basket, shoe cleaning and sewing kits, sun hat, cardboard box with stores for immediate use, tin of biscuits, tray, jars with tea, honey, sugar, peanut butter, milk and egg powder, and that is a catalogue of all my possessions, excepting for a change of underwear and sheets, which recline under the mattress, I have the misguided notion that they may possibly air there, and so feel less like death warmed up when I next have to use them.

The following is from yesterday's *Shanghai Times*, it certainly gives one point of view:

The internment of some 6,000 British, Americans and Dutchmen which started on January 31st is now almost completed. This step has been taken to prevent fifth column activities, and to guarantee stabilized livelihood for the enemy nationals. The enemy nationals are living in camps established in Pootung, Chapei, Lunghua and other suburban districts of Shanghai, with each camp holding from one to two thousand inmates. Religious teachers and hospital workers are being allowed, with special permission, to resume their former work, which is highly appreciated by the individuals concerned as well as by the Chinese public.

All camps are located in quiet suburban districts of Shanghai, and the houses are all well built and in good condition.

Among the internees are those who had lost their jobs with the outbreak of war, and had been wandering aimlessly in the streets of Shanghai. They are now peacefully settled in the camps, many of them are relieved and glad to be in the camps.

The internees are all satisfied and appreciative of the tolerant and considerate treatment given them at the camps. Much attention has been paid to the environment of the internees and to the construction of their living quarters, with meticulous care being given to their food. At the same time ample medical facilities are provided. Inmates are permitted to send and receive letters, they may also read the latest papers and magazines and listen to the radios.

The internees have formed their own committees for the management of their own affairs, and have opened classes for the education of their children.

In order to maintain their health, walking and sport grounds have been laid out where the internees are daily playing tennis and volley ball.

Cultivation of vegetables in the open spaces is another instance of their contented daily life.

Thus the internees are expressing their gratitude for the generous and just treatment accorded them by the Japanese Government authorities, for they are now receiving more protection than ever before.

I hardly know whether to describe it as a passionate under- or over-statement.

This is today's crops of rumours and "Have you heards?" — that we are each to receive an Easter present from the Authorities, *viz*, a roll of toilet paper and a cake of soap. That the canteen is opening within the next few days. That the canteen's opening date is delayed indefinitely. That we are to have special food on Easter Sunday. That one hundred of us are to be allowed out each week to do our shopping in Shanghai. That nobody is to be allowed to go to Shanghai under any pretext whatsoever.

APRIL 25TH. Two days of heavy rain have provided the nearest approach we shall probably ever know to rest and relaxation, with time for comparatively uninterrupted reading, writing and mending. The rain has also given us a holiday from gardening, not unwelcome to aching backs and blistered hands. For gardening here is real he-man's stuff of breaking up grassgrown earth. Coolies were allowed to be hired for a week, just to go over the ground once, but the rain and wind clogs it up again quicker than the spadeworkers can follow, so it has all had to be done again by ourselves. We have to use the great hoes that farmers use, so heavy that at first I could hardly lift one, then we go over with spades, lighter hoes, and for a restful (again comparatively speaking) change, there is the raking and sowing. And all this by the acre. We have already prepared and sown acres of beans, cabbage, tomatoes, corn, cucumbers and pumpkins. I can't think why some gardener hasn't devised some scheme of lifting up the beds to the level of one's waist — anything to make a change from the killing, back-breaking, aching stooping.

One may call the place a Civil Assembly Centre, but it is really nothing but a labour camp, granted that the labour is for ourselves. The men are really beyond all praise. Office workers are transformed into road builders, garbage collectors, stokers, stove builders, hot water firemen, cooks, butchers, and kitchen toilers. Women garden, cook, teach, nurse, clean the dining rooms, clean vegetables, do mending, and dole out the drinking water for hours daily in all weathers — nearly scalded by the steam at their backs, whilst they freeze in front from the howling north westerly winds.

We ALL stand in queues — for meals, for washing water, for drinking water, and for many and various registrations. The latest one being for shower baths. No doubt a shower on alternate days will be a great deal better than none at all, but it all sounds unspeakably exhausting. I have a feeling that I shall continue in the bad old way with a bucket and kettle in the washroom trough, discreetly curtained from the public gaze by my counterpane thrown over a rope — SMELLS from the temperamental cesspool notwithstanding. When I emerge from here I shall always use bath salts, and I'll have grapefruit every morning for breakfast, and cheese every day. And I'll wear soft clinging feminine hostess gowns on every possible occasion, and on impossible occasions too. Three things I shall eschew utterly — messy picnic meals, slacks and bicycles. I can hear you laughing over the first item — that I, the born picnicker should so shamelessly recant.

Camp life is the merciless unveiler of every artifice, whether it be dyed hair, alleged accomplishments or assumed qualities and virtues. The essential personality emerges just as surely as the natural hair colour. As to dyed hair, once a makeshift turban is arranged around the coiffure, we judge that the worst is beginning to happen. And the boasters and assumers of virtues have all become deflated and stripped, and all that remains is the lazy, greedy, dirty or lying residue. And then after all you discover that the liars are often generous, and the greedy ones are very clean, and the lazy ones do leave you in peace.

I am writing this to the accompaniment of strange snatches of conversations as the washroom door opens and shuts, just at my back: ... It's white trimmed with blue.... *Ce n'est que ma lessive.* ... Why the hell not? ... That pipe's blocked again.... I've smashed the only one I had.... Lend me.... Do me a favour.... I'll get some chalk.... I'm so nervous, you can't imagine.... It's fish and cabbage.

MAY 1ST. A limited canteen for the first Assembly opened yesterday. Sales were limited to 1 lb of peanut butter and 1 lb of buscuits per head. Plus one roll of toilet paper from the paternally minded Japanese government. Very useful for cleaning out the greasy frying pan, much in use now that I am the owner of a chattie stove made out of my biscuit tin and some de-barbed wire. I am the proprietary owner seeing that it has been made of my materials and it lives in my corner when not in use, but it is communal in the sense that any one of the five who live down at my end of the hut may use it — coal and wood and paper to be provided by the user. "Provided" is a euphemistic term when it comes to coal and wood, and dire penalties are threatened if more of this "providing" and "finding" goes on.

I will confess to you that I am ashamed to be seen by the Chinese who bring in the supplies when I am grovelling on the ash piles, scratching with a bit of stick for half burned bits of coke and coal. But no doubt I shall outgrow this relic of snobbery. And what is a little shame when it comes to the greatly increased range of food which we can now enjoy? Such luxuries as coffee, pancakes, omelettes, toasted cheese, macaroni, fish cakes, and chocolate pudding or stewed dried fruits. Not to mention the additional conveniences of heated rainwater for hairwashing, odd kettles of hot water or a heated flat iron.

At the same time, during the past few days the official menus have improved as to quality and cooking, and great efforts are being made to vary the sole alternatives . . . stew or fish, with congee or cracked wheat and an occasional egg for breakfast. Tomorrow's breakfast promises to be a perfect gala : congée, egg, and cocoa with milk and sugar. We wonder whether the cocoa has gone mouldy.

Whether it is the hard work or spare living or complete absence of strain and anxiety, I don't know, but I haven't felt as well for months . . . which doesn't in the least mean this is my idea of life. However, if all else fails after the war, surely a Sanatorium run on Civil Assembly Centre lines, for the underworked and the overfed should prove profitable, especially if one advertised it enough and made the charges sufficiently exorbitant.

The final arrangements for the showers have been completed and are pronounced "highly successful." To me they sound unbelievably ghastly and exhausting. Enter bath house on the dot with the 47 other females of your batch, discard shoes, put on clogs, march to locker, undress, the whistle blows and you march to shower cubicle, whistle, water turned on for one minute to wet you, whistle, water turned off, soap yourself, whistle, water on so that you may rinse, whistle, march out and dress, march, change clogs for shoes . . . all to be completed, from moment of entrance to departing wrestle with next incoming queue, in exactly 20 minutes. Oh Lord! how far removed from former hour-long wallowings in

64

hot water with Gardenia bath salts, in fact, from the days when one's bath was "a Period of Relaxation." Meanwhile, as mentioned before, I shall continue with the more individualistic method of bucket, kettle and trough.

NO BATHING ALLOWED IN THESE CLOSETS.

NO DRESSING OR UNDRESSING ALLOWED IN THESE CLOSETS.

DO NOT SPIT. DO NOT LEAVE HAIR IN THE WASHBASINS.

NO MATCHES TO BE THROWN DOWN THE FLUSHES.

NO COTTONWOOL TO BE PUT DOWN THE FLUSHES.

NOTHING TO BE PUT DOWN THE FLUSHES.

DO NOT THROW CIGARETTE ENDS ON THE FLOOR.

COTTONWOOL TO BE PUT HERE. DO NOT BLOW THE NOSE INTO BASINS.

ONLY DISHWASHING HERE. LAUNDRY AND TOILET WASHING HERE.

BATHING ONLY HERE. DO NOT RINSE MOPS HERE. WIPE YOUR FEET.

NO LAUNDRY TO BE DRIED HERE EXCEPT ON RAINY DAYS.

PLEASE LEAVE TOILETS AS YOU WOULD LIKE TO FIND THEM.

All these elementary instructions adorn our washroom walls. You would have thought that most of them would have been unnecessary or self-evident, but apparently they are neither. More than that, one of our inmates announced firmly that she did not mind how dirty the place became, and as she was not used to cleaning out toilets she refused to take her turn. Thank goodness she elected to move out of the hut, and now under our Florence's Lloyd's direction (I think these blessed toilets are her spiritual home) our B West enjoys the reputation of having the cleanest toilets in town. This distinction only gained after much hard work and endless proddings of "The Young" and "The Not So Young" so one can only suppose that all the chalked up legends do eventually percolate.

MAY 7TH. The gardening is getting to be really interesting, and no longer so blindly exhausting now that the back and arms are stronger and the palms nicely calloused. We have been split up into permanent gangs each under a foreman, and allotted an area of ground to cultivate, from original breaking to eventual harvesting. My boss is the suave and elegant, if humourless, Bertie Way transformed, to some extent, since pre-camp days, but still stylish in old shoes, shorts and sweater. There are several congenial men in the gang, such a blessed relief after the concentrated and overwhelming

65

femininity of the hut. At times I loathe the female en masse (self included) — they smell vaguely, and they move around in an aura of bits of washing, cups of cocoa and rubber hot water bags; and endless babble flows from them unceasingly. Gardening with the men one can be so restfully silent, at the end of a furrow one can straighten the back, talk for five minutes about something other than kettles of hot water and flatulence, or how to make a pudding out of nothing — then down the next furrow, and so on, until the three hour shift is over. (N.B. Compare Margaret Halsey's of *Live Alone and Like It* remarks about middle-aged Englishwomen, poor dears, who spend their time gardening and being respected and avoided by Englishmen.)

PARK HOTEL

LIFT OUT OF ORDER.　PLEASE USE THE STAIRS

These two signboards adorn the door of our hut. And here is another, frequently erected *à cause des circonstances plus fortes que nous*:

OUT OF ORDER.　PLEASE VISIT YOUR FRIENDS.

Which no doubt helps us to maintain the before-mentioned reputation for the cleanest toilets in town.

I have recently taken on one hour's work daily at serving drinking water at the newly opened station Waterloo. But unless you should think that this has been done out of pure nobility, I must write you a few words on the subject of Low Cunning and Its Development in Camp Life. I am horrified at my proficiency in the art, and at the amount of mental energy expended on maintaining my high standard in it. I go to bed at night and plan how I can ease my lot next day by judicious employment of L.C. For instance, by getting up at 6 a.m. one can get the most spacious corner of the trough to do the washing with clean fresh water, extra ration of which is granted to all Lady Dippers, (two whole thermos fulls, boiling hot.) Other perks of Lady D's are a pink ticket which enables one to have meals at either sitting (this concession exploited to the full adds greatly to ease in planning the day's activities), showers every day, and buckets of fresh water for hair washing, extra kettles of hot water and teapots filled at odd hours — all these are conveniences well worth the time spent in dishing out water in either grilling sun, clouds of steam, soot and dust, or else in howling gales and floods of rain — with a few pleasant days in

66

between. But to return to low cunning. An early breakfast obtained by the Pink Ticket allows me to head the queue for eggs and fruit at the canteen — time saved and comfort increased. Then again, in order to retain sole use of the only hoe, the head of which does not fly off at the third blow on the ground, I take it home with me, to tiffin, supper and bed, and re-emerge with it next morning when I go gardening. And of course, a few pleasant remarks occasionally to members of the kitchen staff go far towards the collection of stray potatoes, onions and bits of cabbage, for development of dishes cooked on the chattie.

We have been notified today that no radios are to be allowed in any Civil Assembly Centre — probably a healthy symptom, and if it is disappointing in some ways, at least we shall be spared a spate of crooning and crackles. But the flappers are noisily grieved.

It was also decreed that all the heavy baggage belonging to Hut inhabitants which has hitherto been stored in the Assembly Hall must all be cleared out so that a proper canteen, library and kindergarten can be established there. Which means that the trunks will have to come to the huts. As crashes through the floor by bed and chair legs are already of frequent occurrence, the united weight of about 60 additional trunks promises a series of really impressive subsidences — not to mention the frightful congestion down the gangway. (N.B. And farewell to our Fire Chief's favourite game of Daisy Chains with the fire buckets.) A good many feelings were exhibited, both of the audible and inaudible varieties, when this order came out. But when word came that the Japanese Commandant and some gentlemen from Tokyo were coming to visit the huddle, feelings at once gave way to wordless comprehension — certainly we would obey orders and stand meekly by our beds, just as we had obeyed orders and accepted our unwanted trunks — and of course we exchanged courteous greetings — but also, the baggage was so disposed that only by crab-like wriggles could Authority progress upon its way, and where the supply of trunks gave out, there was a sudden mushroom growth of unfolded card tables, camp and deck chairs which impeded all progress. I believe this will be much more likely to bear fruit than any strongly worded protest or active show of resentment.

Tomorrow, our assembly, no: 20 are to get canteen supplies — jam or honey, peanut butter and sweets, eggs at $2 each, and an apple at either 2, 4, 6, or 7 dollars each, according to size. And the paternal government are giving us a piece of soap.

Three more instructions perforce inscribed on the washroom walls:

DO NOT THROW TEA LEAVES IN THE TROUGHS.
THROW TEA LEAVES HERE.
WATER IS SCARCE DO NOT WASTE IT. DO NOT PULL
UNLESS VERY NECESSARY.

MAY 12TH. My 6′ x 4′ is looking as-pleasant-as-possible-under-difficulties since the completion and installation of blue and white check gingham curtains at the windows, and as for my bed, since its adornment with the blue sheets and pillowcases, it is the admiration of the whole dormitory, and the added effect of blue pyjamas calls forth much good-humoured chaff from the passers-by on their way to and from the washroom. It is something new for me to be a leader of fashion, but it is pleasing to have at least one thing different from the 49 others — some lingering flickers of the Individual fighting against being submerged by the mass. Anyway, I chaff back and say that blue won't show the dirt as quickly as white bedclothes, and no tittle-tattle gray for me — but actually I get a strange pleasure as I glide into their cool blueness at night, I can imagine and almost feel cool blue water closing around me, cleansing, refreshing and sweet-smelling. The last adjective is much needed and much missed tonight as the interior cesspool which should have been outside is at its fishiest and cabbageyest, due to the high tides, probably. I hope I never smell that particular odour again, after leaving camp, but if I do, back will flash a complete picture of the place and our existence here.

Summer has arrived, even if one hadn't suspected the fact from the grilling heat of the past two days, the following "Camp Life Vignettes" would confirm the fact. The first caught my eye when I was pinning up my washing on the line this morning at six o'clock. From the next hut, at one of the windows, there was to be seen a leg (female) extended over the sill, receiving the necessary attentions for the wearing of shorts — the wearing of which, is, after all, permitted by Authority. The second one is likely to be a permanency during the whole summer. Our Carmelita, Margy Wooton, ill and diabetic, much loved by us all, spends all her spare time, sitting on a stool by her bed, clad only in a white silk petticoat, legs well apart, just fanning her life away, as she puts it.

The third vision hasn't anything particularly to do with the summer weather, excepting that the heat makes it appear more ridiculous and unpleasant. From the opposite hut again, every morning I can notice the following extraordinary performance. A short and very fat Russian woman, simply dripping in silver fox cape and neckpiece, (these are worn at all hours in all weathers and temperatures) with diamonds as large as Gibraltar upon her fingers, leans out from her window and briskly empties out a little tin into the gutter — she thinks the toilets are too unhygienic.

On today's menu board:

SWEET RICE. BRING YOUR OWN JAM.

Which sounds an Aberdonian way of putting it.

We were talking about the decadence of our table manners and general deportment, and in how short a time the veneer of a lifetime peels off. So for fun I examined my behaviour objectively, and to my horror observed the following: A. An extraordinarily efficient "boarding house reach." B. A running commentary, uttered in a monotonous undertone and addressed to no one in particular, on the food I am in the act of eating — "Eight bits of meat today — cabbage is tough — gravy is good though — congee is raw — cracked wheat burned, as usual — nice egg — " and so on and on. C. In the absence of table napkin, I find that I wipe my fingers upon my bare knees. D. All crumbs are flicked off my plate on to the floor. E. After washing up, all drips are likewise shaken on to the floor during the passage back to the table from the sink, I wonder whether these ghastly habits will trip one up, during a fit of absentmindness, after one returns to civilization, or will one, on the contrary, develop an ultra-gentility of manner, just to be on the safe side. Perhaps even go so far as to crook the little finger when drinking one's tea.

A delightful tale, to my way of thinking. One of the ten little Abrahams, number seven, I think, was getting her water, and Irene Rayden said to her: "I didn't know you were British." "We weren't until there was a B.R.A." (British Residents Association, who helped out greatly, financially and otherwise before we were interned, and during the calling-up period.) A vivid memory of this same Abraham family. As there were the two parents and the ten children, they were assigned a room to themselves. It was an inspiration, a vision of peace and faith to pass by their open door on a Sabbath evening and see the whole family keeping that holy hour — a white cloth on the table, and the seven-branched candlestick; ten as-clean-as-possible children with their mother, and their

69

father intoning the age-old prayers. One was reminded of other days, other worlds, and that this messy phase of life was only an interlude.

I hereby wish to record that I hope I never have to see or fill a thermos flask ever again after I leave this establishment. This bitter reflection the result of a surfeit of filling them daily during the rush hour when I am on water chore — at least 150 of them during that period.

Here are my today's doings. I got up at 5:30 this morning, dressed and did my bits of washing and hung them out on the line, made my bed, swept and mopped the floor, arrived at the head of the breakfast queue by 7:30. Rushed off to Waterloo to get morning ration of drinking water. By 9 o'clock had started gardening, which went on until noon. Exhaustion and hunger drove me to a snack meal. Too tired to cope with another queue for steamed fish and cabbage, so I ate some oddments left over from yesterday, and then instantly collapsed into log-like sleep. Its quality amazes me every time, I never hear a single sound, and yet there is a constant coming and going past my bed, and openings and shuttings of the door. I woke up automatically at 1:45, and went on for the hour's water duty. Got back to the hut at 3 o'clock, covered in soot and dust. Retired to the trough, with kettle and bucket, for nearest possible approach to a bath; it took the best part of an hour before any semblance of cleanliness and polish was noticeable. Then at 4:30 there was Fire Drill. To my consternation found myself ordained Fire Monitor. At 6 p.m. it was time to fix the tray and join in the supper queue, and at 8 I had my Russian lesson. And tomorrow, and tomorrow and tomorrow will be much the same, excepting that if I am not learning Russian, I shall be teaching French at the Polytechnic.

I have great admiration for this institution. One can learn any subject you like to mention — it is really amazing how many teachers of how many subjects are interned here. Already there are classes in French, Russian, Spanish, Chinese — all dialects, German, English language and literature, harmony and counterpoint, astronomy and navigation, physics, biology and botany, mechanics, dress designing — I think the list could go on for ever. And yet, to my fury, I often hear the whiners bemoaning the fact that this internment is just a slice out of their life.

So far the gardening is my main pleasure here, not so much for itself, as for the curious mental state it induces — escape, in a rather

Peter Ibbetsonish[28] manner, from the drabness and monotony, and the eternal babble and coming and going of 1,700 human beings, and from a regimented form of existence. He needed the strait-jacket to escape to his dream world. I find that physical toil, brought to the point of every muscle aching and every joint cracking produces something of the same effect. My mind escapes to its be-loveds — poetry learned, long passages of music I have heard and played, and I can relive, with extraordinary vividness, the happiest hours of my life, that I have spent with you so many years ago. But for the rest of the twenty-four hours, all personal affection, desires, memories or dreams lie in cold storage, submerged under layers of duties, activities and quasi-humorous observation. Only by doing this does this existence become bearable.

Camp organization and improvements have gone ahead with leaps and bounds in the past month. Official rations improve all the time — we even had stewed peaches for breakfast on Sunday. The canteen has enlarged its scope, and now we can get haber-dashery items as well as eggs, apples, jam, honey, sweets, biscuits and peanut butter, on certain days, according to our numbers.

Lunghua Academy, not to be outdone by the Polytechnic, is now in full swing, and doing a wonderful job of work for the three hun-dred odd children. There are concerts, dances, football, hockey and softball matches for those who want amusement and sport. And a Dramatic Society is in process of formation. Flower beds have been laid out, and trees transplanted into clumps and alongside the roads and paths do much towards relieving the uncompromising bareness of the grounds.

MAY 18TH.   After a night of thunderous downpours, I decided that today was a suitable one for a member of the Gardener's Union to take a holiday. So the five of us united in the production of a real breakfast at 9 o'clock — coffee, bacon and eggs, toast and honey.

Then there developed the Saga of the Green Peas, which went as follows:

1. Volunteers called for shelling 2,000 lbs of peas.

2. Kindergarten suspended during pea shelling session, space and teachers both required, with pupils to assist.

[28] A reference to a nineteenth-century novel by G. DuMaurier entitled *Peter Ibbotsen*. The hero, Ibbotsen, was imprisoned for murder but by what was called "dreaming true" he was able to experience liberation.

3. During Classical Concert (gramophone records) still more trays passed along the rows, so that the audience might work whilst listening.

4. Acrimonious dispute between Music Committee and Kitchen Staff as to the propriety of the above arrangement. Compromise reached when back row only of audience allowed to shell, so as not to disturb Classical Enthusiasts in front.

5. Further argument that the back row popping still disturbed Classical Enthusiasts. Back row retorting that they only popped whilst the rain was rattling on the tin roof, so the Classical Enthusiasts couldn't possibly have heard the popping amongst the deafening noise of the rain.

6. Announcement at lunch that volunteers are still needed for pea and bean shelling. Special programme of Light Music provided.

Epilogue.

Neither the peas nor the beans are more than barely eatable due to extraordinary manner of cooking them which transforms each one into a minute leather case containing a slight amount of floury substance.

A corps of women police has been established. Trunks standing in the corridors of the main buildings have been scientifically broken into with skeleton keys, and women are suspected. Heaven knows that I'd hate to lose any of my possessions here, they are so essential and so irreplaceable. But far more I'd hate to have to solve the dilemma I'd find myself in, if I were called upon to hand over the culprit for punishment. One is told that the Herd must be protected, and yet how could one hand over anyone to the Japanese for "questioning" and punishment?

I heard the following delightful remark uttered by one of the kindergarten mistresses who was trying to hold the attention of her outdoor class: "Now, will you pay attention, or do you all wish to grow up into garbage men?" And while she was saying this, two of Shanghai's most notable taipans were passing by, dragging along a garbage truck, chuckling at the irony of the situation. Camp life is such a shake up, and it must be refreshing to all concerned when another taipan is ordered by his former marine superintendant to report in half an hour to unload a truck. I wonder how it will be after the war; all this should make for tolerance and understanding, if only we don't all fall back into the bad old ways.

There are many *"feelings"* over re-measurement and re-allotment of hut space for each occupant and their baggage, so as to allow each person 9 feet by 4 feet, and a clear passage down the middle 4 feet wide. I rejoice, because it has been decreed that my bed cannot be shifted any nearer the wall, otherwise the door will be obstructed — so my hidey corner is saved — there are therefore compensations for slams and smells.

Two of us, both solitude lovers, have designs upon the tool hut which has been erected on our North patch, and which, we feel, belongs equally to us as members of that gardening squad. If only one could retire there by oneself, after work hours, for the sheer bliss of quietness and solitude. One could shut the door, which faces the buildings, and open the window which looks over the ground we have so painstakingly cultivated — and on and on, over the green wheatfields, to the black curly-eaved little houses, which by some optical trick, appear to be swimming in the lovely tender greenness — to the sprays of white field roses growing on the grave mounds outside the barbed wire — and so on — and on — to other days — other worlds — *et toi*.

MAY 26TH. Today I am full of typhoid and cholera inoculations, and consequently, of hatred of the camp and its 1,708 inhabitants. Even today's choicest rumour doesn't seem as funny as it should — we are all to be repatriated beginning June 1st.

It is cold and raining outside, and inside there is a certain amount of bickering — neither will last, but it is unpleasant to have to endure either. I have been thinking that obviously this existence lacks the one essential for making it into a harmonious whole — an all-absorbing idea or conviction to weld together the hundreds of inmates and their individual differences, upbringing and religions and nationalities, such as one would find in a religious establishment, or on a battleship. It seems as if man must have something greater than himself, and beyond himself, to live in anything more than superficial friendliness with his neighbours. Here, apart from frenzied activity on the part of a fairly large majority to the making of the conditions of existence more agreeable, we have nothing that is uniting — unless it is the obsession of eating and the fervent desire to get away from communal life as soon as possible. Now that tiredness and monotony are beginning to feel as though they would last forever, it is a sad but true commentary on human nature to have to remark that the attitude of helpfulness, and the impulses of generosity that helped so much to make our first days here something more than bearable, have now worn very thin.

I am writing to you quite far into the night, as I have to sit up to turn out lights and check in the late comers. Muriel Porter is also played out with chills and inoculations, so her mantle falls upon me. I'm trying to keep awake in the half light until half past ten. The rain outside sounds very soothing and the hut is very quiet, most of the inmates are in bed. Where a whole section has come to an agreement on the subject, the light is off and presumably they are all asleep. Others who wish to sleep while their neighbours still want to read, have their arms flung over their faces (and look as pitiful and vulnerable as do all sleeping adults), or else are burrowed under mounds of bedclothes. One or two are splashing around in the washroom, but it is peaceful enough in my corner, for which I am thankful.

I have had two French classes today, pupils keen and ambitious, but not brilliant, poor lambs. Which doesn't mean I don't enjoy teaching them; indeed grinding through grammar with them has sharpened my enjoyment of the language. And in my rare leisure when I can read, I read only French. And here is a sentence I came upon today, which pleases me and just describes my present frame of mind — it is from an essay by Joseph Jolinnon: ". . . ses mots, qui me reviennent chaque soir au cours de cette brève minute où nous résumons notre destinée, avant de sombrer dans le sommeil."[29]

MAY 30TH, SUNDAY AFTERNOON. I proclaimed today a gardener's holiday, as far as I was concerned, and I planned out a totally different day, as follows: Got up at 5:45 a.m., and cleaned out our lovely new stove and then lighted it, so that Kate Shekury could get on with our Sunday breakfast cooking in between her 7:30 Mass and 10 o'clock water chore. E. and I being engaged on the latter between 8 and 9. Next did my washing, made my bed, served out the drinking water and returned to find toast and coffee and bacon and eggs all ready. From 11 until 2 o'clock I was engaged in a tremendous cleaning out of my — home, do I call it? All very satisfactory and smelling delightfully of soap and disinfectant, though my worst side was aroused by being asked by each person who

[29] "His words, which return to me each evening during that brief minute when we resume our destiny, before falling asleep."

74

passed: "Spring cleaning?" To the first five hundred I meekly replied "Yes," after that, a grunt, and finally, silence.

Then I packed a couple of stale scones, relics of the last party, some biscuits and cold coffee with great secrecy — and to do anything with secrecy here is of unimaginable difficulty — some books, pencil and paper and a rug, and crept out, bound for a secluded spot I had found in the grounds. It was a delightful spot, looking out on to the open country and with a couple of grave mounds to screen one from the hateful buildings and inhabitants. Only encountered two bleaters "Going out?" to whom I answered "No," and eventually reached the quiet spot, more charming than even I had thought, in fact so charming that I felt certain it must be out of bounds — as it happened, that is just what it was. But I had ten minutes of bliss before being courteously but firmly ordered to remove myself. Found it extraordinarily difficult to amble about, as though unconcerned, in order to shake off the Followers and Bleaters so as to reach a second spot, not anything like so delightful as the first, because (a) The only screen consists of young peach trees and silver lamb's tails grass; (b) The Commandant's bungalow is only a couple of hundred yards away, a hideous little red brick bungalow; (c) The hospital is at my back; (d) Two unknown women are secreted under another peach tree to my right, unseen but very much heard — I don't think they can know I am under this tree, judging by the extraordinary scraps of conversation mixed with Bible reading, in unbelievably leaden voices, that are blown to me by the soft fitful breeze. "Traitors — pleasure seekers — whoremongers — St. Paul said — I never did, nothing could be further from my thoughts — mumble, mumble, mumble, then crescendo — I'd like to see any man hold me down in my bed — "

But with all these disadvantages, these two hours — and two more stretch ahead — have been filled with a delight quite out of proportion to the actual surroundings. I have been alone, for the first time since April 4th, 56 days, and to watch the waving grasses, and feel the little peach tree against which I am leaning, swaying in the wind, and to look at the gray sky, and feel the soft damp air, and to be writing to you — all these fill me with a conscious happiness impossible to describe. If one's perceptions and capacity for sensation and appreciation are so sharpened after a few weeks of barrenness, what will they be like after months — or years — when one joins the stream of life again. I can only imagine one will be intoxicated with life and liberty.

JUNE 14TH. Last night we had a gramophone recital, Bach, Haydn and Beethoven, what refreshment after undiluted "South American Way" and "Because" hummed, crooned, whistled and sung by the entire hut, *tutti, a la fuga, solo, duo, largo, allegro,* in tune and out of tune during the past week; all echoes of the Variety Concert. Bach's serene joy, as always, struck me so strongly. Warm, happy faith and simplicity, happy harvest following wise sowing. A beautiful balance with nothing superfluous, a wide-sweeping outline, and such sanity and proportion. Just the antidotes to the trials of camp life. I can completely forget, during the music, the hard bench, cement floors, the sinks with their bleary-looking swabs (the recitals take place in the dining room), the hundreds of faces, nearly all silly looking, my own included, if I could see it — all disappear, and one feels as though one had resumed one's destiny. But the reaction is always the most frightful depression. I can't think how so much beauty can have such an effect; perhaps it is after all because of the spiritual defects in one's make-up.

As from June 1st, we were ordered to sleep under mosquito nets, certainly for our own good, but to hear the grumbles from some of the free-born Britons and others, you would have thought it was a special punishment devised for their greater torment. But in that delightful Proclamation I quoted to you, they forgot to mention in their lyrical enthusiasm over all the Civil Assembly Centres, that Lunghua in particular is a malaria infested swamp. But they have got over the difficulty in a truly Japanese fashion — it has just been officially proclaimed a Malarial Region — which will no doubt go a long way towards draining the swamps and killing the mosquitoes, and providing enough quinine for the future malaria sufferers.

Two days ago we had boiled bacon for breakfast. In ordinary life one might leave it at that, but here it is different. One aspect of camp mentality is the rapid and powerful growth of suspicion, so the first reaction from everybody was "Probably going bad." After receiving my slice I turned it over and over, searching for the expected maggots and there were none. Picked it up and smelled it — delicious! So I ate it rapidly, because it was so delicious, and I refused to be frugal and save half for supper, as I observed many thrifty souls doing.

A great and burning topic during the past weeks has been The Trees. There has been a great deal of planting and transplanting done, which certainly has done something towards relieving the barrenness of the grounds, and has helped in breaking up the uncompromising bleakness of bare straight lines — though I still fervently hope that I shall not have to stay here long enough to be able to enjoy the lovely shade the Pro-Trees so loudly promise for the future. The Anti-Trees thunder about "Waste of Money," it would be "Better to Buy Milk Powder," "Trees Bring Insects," "The trees have cost $2,000." Actually all the trees, about 2,000, are presents, half from the British Residents' Association and the rest from a Japanese friend of Hiyashi, our Commandant, and the cost per head to the 1,700 inmates is $5.

However, this battle has died down in the blood and fire of a new one — the circulation of all money is prohibited as from yesterday. All our private cash has to be turned in to the Civil Assembly Centre Bank, and then it and the long promised, bitterly argued over and just arrived Comfort Fund are to be lodged with a Japanese Bank in Shanghai, all transactions here being done by credit and ledger entries, I can't see that it makes any actual difference, the Japanese occupation C.R.B. currency will crash sooner or later. But to listen to the Voice of the Herd, you'd think we were being robbed at pistol's point. I also notice less enthusiasm over the Comfort money now that it is clear that it is a loan, and not an allowance from the British government.

I have had a flurry of news from beyond the barbed wire, it is good to know that other lives are still flowing along in the outside world. One is only too ready to fall, under the hypnotic effects of the drab routine of internment, into the belief that nothing can be happening outside, and that nobody can possibly still be alive and not in a Civilian Assembly Centre.

The weather is damp and enervating, which reduces us all to the last stages of weariness and depression. The hours of enforced labour are a great physical trial, though without them time would drag, and the depression be all the greater. I should be the last to complain, having put on 9 lbs of weight in two months. But I am pronounced as quite badly anaemic.

JUNE 26TH. In the past two days we have all turned in the last of our cash.[30] A second Proclamation, which left an unpleasing, if vague, threat in our ears. "All offenders will be dealt with accordingly," made one abandon the notion of keeping back enough cash

[30] The author says in 1981, "I successfully kept $1200.00 American Express Cheques in my Elizabeth Arden talcum powder box."

for a rickshaw home. So now for private gambling debts, eggs are our sole currency. One egg — $2.

A beautiful new signboard has been painted by one of our artists, and erected over Dewdrop Inn.

YE OLDE DEWDROP INN.
ALWAYS IN HOT WATER.
BUSINESS HOURS: 7 a.m. to 3:30 p.m.
WATER ONLY SERVED ON THE BOIL.
POCULUM LAETIFICANS SED NON INEBRIANS.

The business is terrific during rush hours. I believe the record was 800 flasks filled in one hour, and a fair average is 400 an hour served by three dippers. We are united in our hatred of thermoses of all sizes and kinds — big, little, wide necked, narrow necked, wooden, tin or basket covered.

An elaborate system of checking the rations has been evolved, which occasioned the usual display of feelings for the first day or two, but the result has been an economy of 300 gallons a day. A great saving, seeing that it has all to be brought in from Shanghai; sometimes the truck makes three trips daily. The decrepit state of the truck, and the fearful disrepair of the roads make one wonder how long this can be kept up.

That such a system of checking should be necessary, is a dreary commentary on camp mentality and private acquisitiveness, and not very flattering to human nature. It appears necessary to have to run a private detective agency when dealing with Food or Privilege in any form, in order to keep one step ahead of scheming minds. In this case, the vigilance, and consequent economy have resulted in a 50% increase of the daily water rations, we now get 4 pints each (1 pint requisitioned by the kitchen).

The following could be called an essay on the futility of attempting to own private property whilst in camp. In an access of nostalgia for something really my own, I decided, about a week ago, to cultivate a private garden under my window. Total footage, 6 x 3, tomatoes, 4 beetroots, 1 sprig each of mint and parsley, 1 pumpkin, 3 cannas planted against the fire water kong, a poplar sapling, and 1 cucumber climbing round my window. For a couple of days the sense of ownership was very strong and pleasureable, in spite of having to drag up buckets of water from the pond. And I even went the length of getting a board inscribed:

78

in an effort to protect the plants from buckets of suds or disinfectant water negligently flung from the washroom door. And then
came the FLOOD. For one afternoon we were wading knee deep in
water, myself wearing bathing suit and gumboots, dredging for
bricks, which were passed along a chain line into the hut to be
placed under our baggage, in case the typhoon continued and the
water rose further — already the floor boards were damp. And the
board mentioned above was to be seen floating up and down, with
a hint of irony on its face. When the flood subsided, a few of the
plants were holding up their heads, but I feel as though I Have
Done With Private Property For Ever.

As I am writing this, "the Very Young" are all tittivating for
the fortnightly Saturday dance. Such a rushing and twittering and
giggling amidst an aura of talcum powder — rather gallant the
show they manage to make under difficulties and the limitations of
our surroundings. But I, for the first time, realize that 40 must be
middle age! A cement floor, two banjos and a piano, and a scarcity
of males is a combination which fails to produce in me the least
thrill as far as dancing is concerned. I'd need the flowers, the gown
and slippers and jewellery, the music, lights and partner — you can
just see how difficult and exacting middle age is. As it is, I am
looking forward with pleasure to the couple of hours of near silence
and almost deserted dormitory lying ahead.

I notice that our Kate has retired within her mosquito net,
accompanied by her major consolations — a pack of cards to tell
her own fortune, and her prayer book, in preparation for Mass
tomorrow morning. An excellent strategic position, enabling the
best possible use to be made of both worlds. And also certain signs
that she too is victim of the all-pervading depression.

For nothing in the world would I want you to have to live
through internment, but if only we could laugh together at the
ridiculous nothings that pass for humour here. For instance there is
Bobbie and her favourite words: "I'm getting organized" — and
after we had laughed her out of that expression, "I'm getting ad-
justed" — applied to every situation from tidying up her corner to
general conditions of internment. I have capped the words on her
behalf, by using "co-ordinated," which sounds sufficiently pompous
and ridiculous to reduce those of us who are honoured members of
the Looney Bin to helpless laughter. I may add that the Looney

Bin-ites, with their witty, if low, backchat, and consequent laughter, are a source of envious wonder to "the Very Young," who inhabit the other end of the hut. No doubt they wonder what we poor old ladies with one foot in the grave can possibly find to laugh at, at this latter end of our lives, themselves taking life very seriously, when they aren't dressing for the dance.

Then there is Mamma Gast and her wheedling "Darling . . ." and when the thumb and forefinger go up, one trembles, because the dear only knows what she wants to borrow (if you can call it borrowing!) but it is sure to be something. ". . . Just one onion, darling . . . your fire . . . a few tea leaves . . . just a little box of matches . . . some hot water . . . your bucket . . ." An irresistable old rascal, quite conscious of her lazy roguery, which is entirely redeemed by great kindness and boundless good nature.

And seeing that this letter has already told you about the Saturday night entertainment for "the Very Young," what do you say to this as a festivity for one "Not So Young?" It is one that requires skill, patience and forethought, and is essential from time to time, thanks to camp diet, both official and private. I refer to the taking, or should it be the enduring of an enema. It has to be on Saturday night because of the Dance ensuring some degree of solitude, instead of endless Bangings on The Door. It requires organization, because both hot and cold drinking water have to be accumulated for the occasion, so I behold myself retiring, laden with 1 kettle of cold water, 2 thermos flasks of hot, the apparatus, and a mosquito coil — for the nether regions are simply infested — and the dormitory knows me not for half an hour or so. But there being neither privacy nor reticence in camp life, upon my return, looking rather less like a gasometer than usual, up goes the ribald chorus: "She's debeaned . . . !" And I laugh too, and hate and loathe the squalor and want of privacy until I can discover something else ridiculous to laugh at. I think an ability to clown helps one along from day to day more than anything else. I don't say it is the most lofty method, but it is the one that gives one least heartsickness.

JULY 7TH. Yesterday I got my first letter from you since October 1941. I wonder if I can tell you what it means to know that there still exists anything so stable, so unchanging as yourself and the life you lead, within a world that at present holds almost nothing upon which one can depend. All yesterday I could have sung for joy, and I certainly boasted to everyone that MY letter had only taken

Refuge from Typhoon in Assembly Hall — the morning after!

Washing at the Trough

West Kitchen — "A" team at work

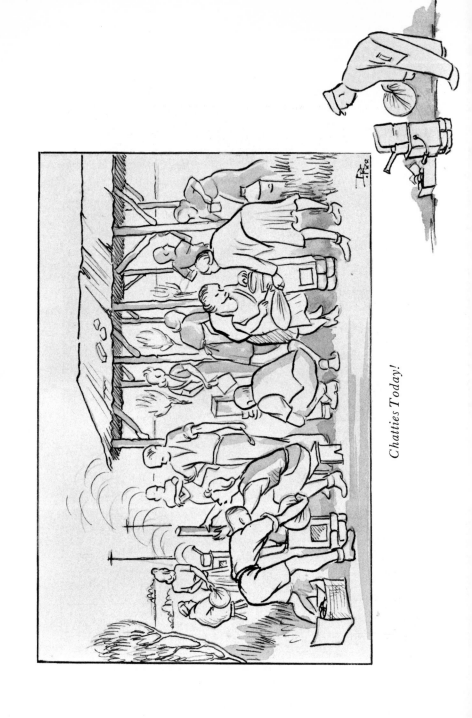

Chatties Today!

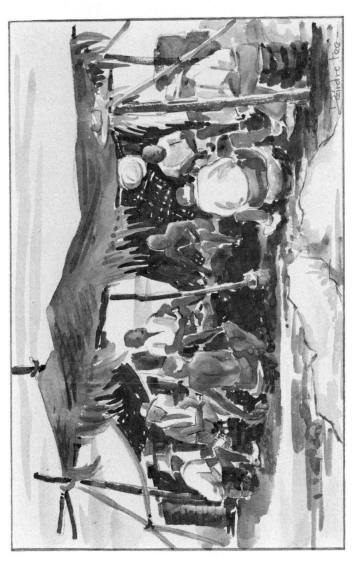

T'ai-p'ans' Corner — P.W.D. breaking bricks for road-making

"*Waterloo*"

Recreation Ground — "Kitchen v. Hot Water"

My Corner of the Hut

eighteen months to arrive, compared to theirs of two years, and others were boasting to me of some remarkable feature in THEIR letter. And today the reaction has set in — I suppose the last in the world that you would expect. But I have noticed that after every influx of mail, the most appalling depression sets in. It is something so bad, that the accepted etiquette is just not to speak to anybody who has just had a letter — just leave them alone until they have had time to bury their emotions again. And so it is with me today — I could just cry with misery. And at the same time, I can picture you straining every muscle to get letters to me. I can see you besieging the authorities, to try and find the quickest and best way of getting letters here, and I can hear you saying "As long as I can get letters to her, she'll keep her courage and spirits." How you will laugh when you read this. And meanwhile, I love having your letter, but I am thankful they don't come often enough to make a permanent poor fish of me.

As well as letters, the Red Cross brought in our monthly parcels from our contacts in Shanghai. Parcel day is always a great excitement, something like prize giving at school. The children are always the first to see or hear the lorries lumbering along the main road, before they turn into our private lane. And from them the cry goes up, to be caught and carried along by all and sundry "Parcels . . . parcels" and then they are unloaded by our Camp Service men, and carried into the dining rooms, there to be searched by the gendarmes, and a few hours later, we are allowed in to collect them. That same evening, all over camp and in every corner, parties are in progress. This state of affairs continuing for a few days, the entertainments decreasing in lavishness as the supply of fresh cooked food, fruit and cakes dwindle. We then return to thinking that our meals concocted on the chattie are the best the world can offer. I must say they have greatly improved along with our skill in getting the chattie to burn successfully — this last only at the price, I am sure, of leaving camp with the right arm considerably larger and more muscular than the left, from having had to spend so many hours fanning the wretched stove. But the menus certainly include such ambitious sounding dishes as salmon loaf, cracked wheat, soufflé, black onion soup, custards, frying pan cakes and pies.

Kate's cards must have been propitious; she has just announced another spasm of "Feelings in Her Bones" — and undoubtedly a cool and dryer breeze is beginning to blow at my window, so maybe things will begin to look up again — and a new crop of camp rumours will start circulating. Last week's efforts were so glorious and flamboyant that I cannot imagine why the war is still going on, or why we are still here.

JULY 10TH. Two days ago we had a visit from our Protecting Consul, Emil Fontanelle. It *would* be a fine day, and he came at one of our more leisured moments, in fact we were having a tea party under Irene's striped garden umbrella, and by walking quickly through the grounds you could almost imagine yourself at some rather rough holiday resort. If only he had come when it is cold and wet, and we are huddled upon our beds, with damp outer clothes lying about, waiting to be put on at any moment. And our wretched washing is festooned everywhere, without the least hope of it ever getting dry until the next fine day. And the mud lies almost as thick upon the floor of the hut as out of doors, and the toilets are blocked up — as they always seem to be in wet weather. And the water is all turned off. But even so, I daresay, it looked pretty ghastly to them, coming straight from their well-ordered homes. We have got more or less used to the squalor. Looking at them I was reminded of the time I was taken to see the Jewish refugee camps down in Hongkew, before the Pacific War, in the remote days when one was well dressed and drove in a car. I remember I was so ashamed to be watching the poor herd huddled up amongst their boxes and washing lines, standing in queues, and falling over each other for want of space, and living in all that ugliness and noise and want of privacy — just as we are now — that I who had everything, could not look them in the face.

The nicest thing that has happened since I came here is that I have acquired a cat — and with official blessings, which is more than I would ever have expected. Actually the rat situation has been getting beyond bearing. Can you believe it when I tell you that several of this hut's inmates' sweaters and dresses, which they laid on their chair or bed whilst they were asleep, have, during the night, had great holes eaten out of them by rats? And every night the rats hold steeplechases along our shelves, gaily knocking over flasks, getting inside tins and eating anything they can get their paws on. So the Health Department sent out to Shanghai, and a mixed basket of cats was sent in. I picked out an elderly black lady about to have a family, a poor frightened thing, with a big bite on her back, but so grateful for any kind word. Her wretchedness makes me feel a Queen of the Earth in comparison — which is good

82

for the morale. And it now gives me pleasure to come home from work, and find in my corner some creature who is glad to see me. She is terrified of everyone else, and spends all the time I am absent, buried in the remotest corner under my bed.

An odd form of malaise is making itself felt, which for want of a better name, we call "campitis." It manifests itself by a sprain in this one, an ache in that one, vague fevers and upset tummies, and an all-pervading tiredness.

Just as I was wondering if I would ever be rid of these aching muscles and bones and the feeling of being drowned in an ocean of weariness, deliverance has come in the form of a strained tendon, which necessitates keeping my leg up. Thank heaven for the respite from physical labour. I can't begin to describe the bliss of being completely idle, lying on my bed, watching the trees, the grass and the clouds. I devise vague plans of studying hard at the Russian, sewing and mending the various wreckages of garments — and I do nothing — and my bones and muscles don't ache. My neighbours are perfect loves, they get my water, do my washing and fetch my meals, etc. I feel vague compunctions when I remember their muscles and bones are feeling just as mine did, their feet as flat and their arches as fallen, and whilst reflecting, I fall asleep.

All this is such a change from the chasing after one's tail of yesterday afternoon. After lunch I agreed with myself that the floor around my bed needed sweeping. Whilst reaching for the broom, poor Topsy emerged from under the bed and explained that she wished to be fed. Last night's meat found to be bad in spite of makeshift refrigerator (Jeremiah Esq., filled with salt water). Enquiries from the kitchen produced negative results — meat not yet arrived from Shanghai. Raw egg beaten up satisfied her immediate pangs. Journey to garbage can with egg shell. Wash and wipe up saucer. Time to reorganize water from thermos flasks into bucket, so as to have both hot and cold water for drinking and washing. Floor still unswept! Time to fix tea. Teapot found to be full of stale tea leaves. Trip to garbage can to empty same. Not enough bread for toast so decided on sliced cucumber. Another trip to garbage can with the peelings. Washed up tea implements. News that the meat had arrived. Trip to kitchen to collect some scraps. Fed Topsy. Washed saucer. Another trip to the garbage can with piece of scorned gristle. Floor still unswept! Tidied bed, and again reached for brush and dustpan, when the cry went up that the newspaper had arrived — and here unless you read it the moment it comes, it may be hours before you see it again, if you ever do. The offer of a spare bucket of hot water produced further spasms of organization so as to manage to wash both my clothes and myself. Time to prepare hoarded vegetables into a salad, as they would otherwise spoil. Washing up of utensils used. Floor still unswept! and by this time ankle deep in dust, and crumbs. Topsy needed to be enticed out of doors — being new to the hut, and in her "delicate state," her outings need organization. Supper time. Time to bring in washing from the line, fold it up and put it away. And then I swept the floor. And then I went to bed.

My poor Topsy has disappeared today. I hope it only means that she has discovered a corner to her liking because with all her meekness on other subjects, she has retained enough catly arrogance to scorn the basket with hay, prepared under difficulties, for her accouchement.

JULY 10TH. Overheard from the Washroom. "... Miss Lloyd the window WAS open, and I told her that it was bad for my rheumatism, but some people are so selfish, only think of themselves. So I shut it and told her that I'm quite willing to have it open when it is really hot — and I know when it is really hot — but some people are so selfish, never think of others. . . ."

Irene Rayden is also suffering from "campitis," her form being tummy, fever and throat so though we are both feeling languid, our lowish senses of humour devised the infantile amusement of counting the uses to which we put Jeremiah Esq. The most important fact is, that, as with so many other implements necessary to camp life, he is *never* used by us for the purpose for which the Lord intended him. But he is invaluable in his capacities of wash basin, for oneself, clothes or dishes, as refrigerator, salad bowl, flower bowl, cheese dish, pickle jar, biscuit canister, bread bin, flour bin, soiled linen container, shopping basket, water storing receptacle, sauce pan, and with the lid reversed, as pedestal for one's mosquito coil. But above all, he is the receptacle, *par excellence*, for mixing one's cake batter, you get such a gorgeous grip of the handle, and then beat like mad.

While the two of us are malingering agreeably, at the top end of the hut there are two genuinely sick girls, malaria with a vengeance, both of them 106 today. We encourage them by telling them that they'll be normal tomorrow, and bad again the next day, and normal the day after that. This is the normal course of the Lunghua variety. And the callous sounding remarks just show you what we have come to. When the first two victims came down with 105 fevers, we were horror-stricken, and the owners of a screen and strip of red carpet swiftly placed these luxuries around the sufferers beds, and we all talked in hushed whispers, but already, the *empressement* has worn thin, and the carpet and screen remain at their owners bedsides, and we all talk cheerfully, and heartily, encourage the sufferers, knowing that in all probability it will be our turn tomorrow.

Unless you should think that this letter is only going to talk about sickness, here are two delightful howlers perpetrated by two pupils of Lunghua Academy.

"Henry VIII had a daughter called Elizabeth, who was later known as Bloody Mary."

"Henry VIII got tired of his wife Katherine, so he sent her to Cardinal Wolsey to try her."

And an overheard conversation between two boys:

"What was your report like" "Awful, and yours?"

"Rotten." "And Jack's?" "Rotten." I know what it is, the masters here aren't paid, so they tell the truth."

This afternoon we were asking our newest inmate, who came in with last week's Assembly, what was her impression upon joining us veterans of four months standing. She said she could only think of *The Grapes of Wrath*, and that she had come to live with the characters of that book. She had been prepared for enamel plates and mugs, but the sight of each of us diving into jam or peanut butter jars with our knives filled her with horrified amazement. But I notice she has become already as good a diver as any. All the same I suppose we do look an appalling gang to any clean and tidy newcomer, fresh from a home, with the graces of life still fresh in their memories, and therefore showing in their actions.

JULY 20TH. The great heat is upon us. If only one could be really clean, and have no physical chores, the least of which is completely exhausting — in other words, if one wasn't in camp, a summer at Lunghua would be very agreeable, at least 10 degrees cooler than the city. But being as we are, it needs every ounce of self control not to blaze up in irritation at the flies, the noise, the smells, the crowds, the scarcity of water, the perspiration, and the unappetizing stews during the day, and at night, the rats and mosquitoes. And at all hours overwhelming tiredness. I believe half the minor accidents, which are increasing in number daily — here a tumble, there a cut hand, or a bad scald, and all the sprains and strains are due to the clumsiness which comes from fatigue, plus some kind of mental lethargy. I am on light duty these days, as water scrutineer for two hours daily — a sitting down job, and I am so tired I can hardly speak. Dear knows what I'd be if the blessed knee hadn't gone back on me.

I have devised a suitable motto for the Lunghua coat of arms, if one is ever designed:

Every Job Has Its Perks.

For instance, the Bath Attendants get longer showers, unharried by blasts of the whistle, I had serious thoughts of turning to this profession whilst gardening is forbidden. In this heat its Perk sounded so tempting, but the daily sight of all those hot and unbeautiful female bodies was too high a price to pay.

Then the Hospital Aides have access to the sole Frigidaire within reach of the Imperialists — the others are all devoted to the Co-Prosperity Sphere. I am happy to say that our Babbie, having tried several jobs, and hated them all, is now a Hospital Aide, so ice cubes are not unknown in our corner (with consequent feverish organization and decanting) so as to have one thermos filled with cold drink. The Dining Room Servers lay aside the more tempting portions, and larger shares of any occasional luxury such as cucumber or peanuts, for their own consumption. The Lady Dippers contrive extra flasks of water. The Vegetable Workers, raw vegetables. The Kitchen Workers, extra bread, and oil for frying — and so on. All a source of a lot of chaff, and I believe, quite harmless, so long as it is done and acknowledged openly. In fact, if you sin, at least be open and joyful about it. But there is a certain element here, who regale themselves with the perks in a coy and cheerless manner and swoop with unholy glee upon the merry if unrepentent "Perkers."

I have to laugh at the muddle surrounding me as I write — even though it nearly drives me mad. Its sole redemption is that it is a logical muddle, caused by having as many of the things I MAY need within reach, so as to save the knee. I still have to rest it as much as possible and avoid all unnecessary movement — instructions which I take to only too gladly. I am on the bed, propped up with pillows piled against a wardrobe trunk at the bed head, the sleeping mat is slippery, if coolish, which complicates the keeping in position if the contraption for keeping the Leg Up — Babbie's sleeve board wedged into Ena Shekury's stool. Lying in disorder on the bed are the fan and inevitable fly swatter, a mosquito coil burning on the lid of a food container, Russian grammar, exercise books and pencils, a *Life of Rembrandt*, Longman's French grammar, sewing apparatus, tray with supper contrived by myself — the food trying to keep itself cool in a Jerry full of salt water, and lastly, the washboard supporting the notebook I am writing in. And I hereby wish to record that one can lose more things per square inch on a bed than anywhere else in the world. My whole vista is cluttered up with such hot and unpleasant articles such as the greasy bit of bacon wrapped in muslin hanging from the curtain rod at the open window just weeping tears of fat in this breathless heat. The array of pots and containers standing in coolish water trying to keep the cat's food from going sour or bad between one meal and the next.

Topsy produced her family five days ago, under the shelf at the head of Caté's bed, an occurrence not welcomed by her, but borne with better grace and more fortitude than I would have expected. Yesterday I removed mother and children to my corner, and one of my greatest pleasures is in watching them — an effortless occupation well suited to my present spineless condition. Gloria, the cow, having conveniently produced a calf a few days ago, my Topsy gets a nightly ration of milk, and what she can't finish inevitably goes sour during the night, so, being in camp, I make a spoonful of cream cheese out of it. A case of me living off my cat instead of my cat living on me. Reminds me of Samuel Pepys Junior and his diary of the 1914 War.[31]

A deluge of rain has just started, and it has induced our Beauty Chorus to put on their bathing suits and go outside with a cake of soap apiece. I can see them all in a lather, hair, arms and legs. One way of having a shower unharried by the whistle.

AUGUST 11TH. A typhoon has been raging since 5 a.m. We hope it reached its peak half an hour ago — 4 p.m. Under enormous difficulties we worked at Dewdrop Inn for a couple of hours this

[31] A reference to a book published in World War I which was a pastiche on Samuel Pepys, the seventeenth-century diarist. In *Pepys Junior*, the author, noting a shortage of food, was forced to use food allocated for pets and it was a reverse of roles, the writer living off the pet instead of vice versa.

morning, so a few hundred got a ration of water. The roof was blowing off in sections, screens flying and ourselves half drowned. Got back to the hut to find that water and electricity had been cut off, and the roof of the West dining room and its ceiling had gone, and a section of the Assembly Hall was going. As always in an emergency, the men were beyond praise, struggling up to the hut roofs, in the torrents of rain and the gale, trying to tie down, with lengths of our trunks' ropes and washing lines, the flapping sheets of corrugated iron. As each hour passed reports circulated of this roof and that wall going.

An emergency squad brought our mid-day rations on push carts to each of our billets. All afternoon we heard (to be quite honest, I didn't hear, I slept, with the frightened cat and oblivious kittens snuggled close to me) the howling wind and the rain thundering on the roof, sheets of iron and pieces of wood banging, and blowing on the wind like bits of paper, bamboo matting and straw floating around on the small sea, which is all that is visible of our gardens. And then the cries: "C West has gone, A East has gone, B East has gone," it seemed impossible that our roof could hold out. But it did, except for some leaks, that could be dealt with by means of basins and buckets. And then the refugees from B East came in, the men helping them with their mattresses, bedding, nets, chairs, crockery, suitcases, bundles and baskets full of clothing, bottles and tins, all dumped on to our beds and on to every available inch of the floor. It would need some great caricature artist to give an idea of the welter. Some of the owners were quite cheerful, some looked as though they had been shipwrecked, but all were amiable. A sudden gust of wind would shake our roof and walls ominously, and we had the consoling knowledge that if the worst happened we would never be able even to reach our belongings, let alone save them, as they were buried deep under the refugee things. I have one quarter of my bed free, if you can call it free, with the cat family and myself parked thereon. The rest is covered with two mattresses and bundles of bedding, owners unknown. Topsy's basket is full of bottles, crockery, food and cutlery, and my window corner is stacked with three baskets of someone else's possessions, and two bundles belonging to another unknown refugee.

In the midst of it all, our Pat and Vera, perfect heroines, flushed the toilets by hand, and so relieved a painful situation. We certainly look like Orphans of the Storm. If only the dapper Emil Fontanelle could see us now, instead of when we were eating lettuce for our tea under a striped garden umbrella.

AUGUST 12TH.　The typhoon blew for twenty-six hours. It is now just an ordinary gale. Last night was an unforgettable experience. From 1 o'clock to 4 the wind and rain were terrific, and we gave up hope that the roof could hold any longer. But excepting that the leaks grew bigger, and one sheet of iron got partly loosened and clanged monotonously above the noise of the storm, it remained intact. The interior of the hut looked like a dungeon, our only light coming from one storm lantern and an electric torch, with the piles of refugees' things lying everywhere, and the gaunt shadows flickering on the wall and the appalling noise outside, it suggested to me one of Doré's illustrations for [Dante's] Inferno come to actuality.

Irene and I, being wise virgins, had gone to bed fully clothed in shirts and shorts. The others, who had undressed, got up around one o'clock and started dressing and packing rather aimlessly — a strangely unreal scene in the darkness — playing shadows and feeble lantern light.

Muriel Porter, very businesslike and untiring in her efforts, both in trying to keep up the failing spirits, and in keeping an eye on windows and doors, to see that they were holding.

Carmelita and I consider we were exemplary as assistant monitors. By continuing to lie in bed and do nothing, we hoped we were radiating an atmosphere of calmness.

I had the cat and kittens inside the net with me, in case we had to do a bolt, and their warmth and obliviousness to the noise was very comforting. In the same way one felt very safe under the net, it felt like an extra roof between oneself and the storm.

We were a pale and exhausted-looking crew this morning, but we all revived when the men, bless them! arrived with buckets of hot water for us to wash in, and later they returned with our breakfast rations, tea and cracked wheat. The poor souls from the wrecked huts had spent a miserable night in the Assembly Hall, cold, wet and mosquito bitten. The Commandant, Mr. Hiyashi, was very concerned and did his best to console them by serving out a tot of saki to each one.

It was interesting and amusing, as always, to observe the essential individual emerging from each person during this crisis. The grasping mother whining for second helpings for her young child before we had all even had our firsts — I suppose she would call it ma-

89

ternal love! Another invited three refugees and all their bundles to share the hospitality of her bed, and the moment the roof really sounding as though it were going, she turned them and their belongings off in a heap because she had to pack her own things. But others were marvels of generosity and forbearance, and shared their space, their food and their possessions.

The wreckage is too pathetic, after all the work and effort that has been expended in an effort to make the place a little more attractive. Trees are down, flower-beds washed away, paths inches deep in mud and debris, mat sun sheds gone, gaping holes in the roofs.

Hiyashi went to town to requisition a repair squad, and this is what turned up — or so the story has it — twelve men with four hammers, who, when they saw the chaos, uttered "Ai ya," and returned to town. In addition we were supposed to have fed them out of our rations and to supply them with all building materials. I take it that our next Comfort Money will be earmarked "For Repairs."

SEPTEMBER 13TH. The light and water are on again, and what mercies they are. For days we had had to depend on what water we could draw from the well, a wearisome process carrying every bucketful. And between you and me, I am lost in admiration for anyone who can throw a bucket into the well, and whilst not forgetting to hold on to the rope, knows how to beguile the bucket into assuming the right way up position. Whenever I tried, the wretched thing's bottom bobbed insultingly at me — it wouldn't even lie on its side. Well now we can be reckless with water again — relatively speaking, instead of having to make one bucket do for washing oneself, one's essential garments, dishes, mop the floor and flush the toilet.

SEPTEMBER 17TH. The news of Italy's capitulation gave me a joyful *idée fixe* during the alternate burnings and freezings of Langhua malaria. So much better than the hobgoblins that sometimes haunt one in high fevers. According to schedule I was up and around, though very tottery, after three days, and today I am resting under R's mat shelter, alone, in the lovely autumn air, and fresh breeze, it is unspeakable bliss. I find that my mind and memory are beginning to stir and fumble about, like a child beginning to walk, after the past weeks of depression and lethargy — an only too prevalent state amongst us all, for no special reason, excepting the general one of wanting to go home.

And I have to admit that I have developed as pleasant a routine as possible, under the circumstances, with light duties as scrutineer at Waterloo and Dewdrop. Very congenial companionship with Willie Way every evening for outdoor supper made from our united parcels cooked by me on the chattie, and from thence being squired to whatever the evening offered, whether lecture, concert or just pleasant talk up on the cool roofs of E or F buildings. But the fact remains, old jokes are wearing out, and show the irritations beneath. General weariness makes a potential "old soldier" out of everyone; the suggestion of an extra chore calls forth fervent protestations of "no time," and "unfair . . . so and so uses it just as much as I do, so why should I be called upon." etc., etc.

I also notice that even the most sceptical of us love to be comforted by fortune telling, whether by hands, cards or tea leaves, or dream books — anything so long as we are promised early deliverance from the monotonous pointlessness of camp life. Rumours are the breath of our life, we don't even ask for truth. But the funny thing is that many of the wildest of them do come true with the passage of a little time, as for instance, Italy's surrender, the scuttling of the *Conte Verde* and *Lepanto*. Which makes me pretty sure that there is a useful little box, shall we call it? somewhere in the camp.

I think too, that some of the general depression dates from the time the evacuation ship left, taking with it some twenty or so of our inmates, who qualified according to the exchange terms. But if, as I told you, letters from the outside world have that odd depressive influence, you can imagine how we who are left behind feel, when we know that some who have been here are well on their way to freedom. The poor dears had a terrific time getting away, with not less than three fine toothcomb examinations of their baggage. Notwithstanding the Co-Prosperity Sphere's thoroughness, I have reason to believe that the Imperialists were, in some cases, one step ahead. Nothing written or printed was allowed to be taken, whether it was the labels on medicine bottles, address books, inscriptions in Bibles, reading matter of any kind, letters or notes.

The compound, formerly occupied by the military who just folded up their tents and stole silently away one early morning, has been turned over to our use. This should relieve some of the chaos and congestion produced by the typhoon. There is talk that the

91

school can be removed there bodily from its present odd holes and corners.

This morning I watched an almost unbelievable sight, namely 50 coolies transporting a whole wooden hut on their bamboo poles, the general effect being that of some gigantic scorpion trotting along the main road! It struck me again, with what facility the Chinese work. They lift and carry with apparently no effort, where we rush and strain and groan, hence the sprained joints and backs, broken arms and legs amongst us. At any rate, the sight of that hut jogging along, with a hundred feet visible, all trotting in time to the "ee haw, ee haw," cheered me up after having made the painful discovery that my mosquito net was bug-ridden. Note the sad decadence, the pain was not on account of the bugs, but because of the awful labour involved in getting the net washed and dried.

Here is the first verse of the Litany I have composed, in a fiercer access than usual of irritation at the noise and the flies in the hut:

"From loud lamentations, scoldings and disputings
in shrill female voices, from recriminations,
complaints and looks of smug triumph,
Good Lord Deliver us."

This all sounds very peevish, and there are brighter sides to life! I find that I waste hours of this convalescence watching the graceful movements of the enchanting daughter that Topsy produced, a black and white kitten, called Mandy because she reminds us all of a panda, I can't really follow the train of reasoning, but there it is. Anyway it is a delightful occupation, whilst eyes are too full of aches to do much reading or writing at a time.

And here is another Camp Vignette which would make you laugh — perhaps will make you laugh when you read this, some day. Kitty Lant is a pugnacious little Irishwoman, with a heart of gold, and the most vivid imagination in the world. She has just emerged from being fitted with complete top and bottom dentures, she has just been telling me all about them, and to illustrate how much she disliked them, she removed them, and held them up and gesticulated with them, almost thrusting them into my face, and all the while carried on an endless tirade about the misdemeanours of all dentists in general, and our dentist in particular. Between my gulps of supressed laughter, I uttered soothing little noises, fortunately no coherent remarks were required.

And here is a picture of real nobility. The A.C.S. Dean Trivett and all the Reverends have constituted themselves as the Drains Trust. I can't describe to you what a ghastly job it is, and yet every morning they go round, poking out the septic tanks, none of which work properly, with lengths of split bamboo, while we push at our end with old mops, this delightful performance has to go on, until there is a faint but encouraging gurgle in the pipes. We then collapse, but those stout-hearted men just move on to the next blocked up horror.

SEPTEMBER 27TH. I have changed my occupation since last writing to you. I am now a fully fledged French schoolmarm, with nineteen classes weekly, all ages, from 7 to 70. The elder ones come to the Polytechnic classes, and the others I teach in the school. Great changes have occurred there, it has been moved *en bloc* to the "New Territory," to the buildings recently vacated by the military. And with all the deficiencies and drawbacks, it is a great improvement on trying to give classes in the dining rooms and in odd corners of the Assembly Hall or out in the grounds.

The school buildings have been pretty badly damaged as a result of the last war, and the soldiers who have been living there have contributed their share of dirt and destruction. Windows are badly broken, and small chance of being able to replace more than a few panes. The carpenter's shop have knocked together rough tables and benches, and so now we are off — with about one textbook to eight children, barely enough exercise books to give each child one, not enough pens, pencils, ink or chalk — but we are off!

I love teaching the seven year olds, and those in their late teens, but for sheer unmitigated gangsterism, commend me to Form IIB! If ever an innocent was thrown into the lion's den, it was me on the first morning I was set to instruct them in the rudiments of the French tongue. However, I am happy to say, that now the tables are firmly turned, and one of my fellow teachers told me today that Form IIB are now afraid of me.

Yesterday we had our first escape from the camp. I still daren't hope that the rest of us will escape punishment, but so far we have only been forbidden to walk anywhere near the barbed wire fences, and only the escaper's wife and close associates have been questioned. The rumour today is that the Commandant sent for Mrs. C. and said: "Mrs. C. you are now a widow." But we don't believe they have caught him even, much less killed him. If they had, they would surely have given themselves the sadistic delight of parading him amongst us, and probably executing him before our eyes.

This afternoon a large batch of men arrived here from Pootung, ostensibly to help with the heavy work of this camp which is heavier even than in the other camps because of the water situation, and also because of the great distances involved between building and building, our whole area being much greater than any other Civil Assembly Centre. As I say, the ostensible reason is to help with the heavy work, but we do hear rumours that Pootung won't be sorry to see the last of some of the lads. And I must add that amongst these arrivals are several answers to Lunghua maidens' prayers. At the time when applications were invited by the Japanese for all who wished to have relatives moved from other camps to wherever the "applier" was interned, there went forth a spate of petitions from here, for the transfer of relatives of all degrees, for boy friends, and one young lady, just to be different, asked for her "Guardian," which somehow made us all laugh. (N.B. My friend Willie Way has been designated as "Carter's Custodian" so there shall be no misunderstanding by the B West inmates.)

Well, all this has provided some welcome breaks, and has helped to lift us out of the poultice of depression under which we all slumped after the repatriates left for home. Now we shall resume the old pendulum swing between tremendous elation, (born of Lunghua rumours, some of which come true) and a pessimism which cannot visualize our release at any period short of another five years with a dogged, rather lethargic state of mind at the middle.

NOVEMBER 23RD. It is hard to explain the long gap between my last letter to you and this one. Part of the reason is just plain idleness (mental only) and partly it is because the day in and day out round only leaves one with leisure when one is too tired to use it in any other way than in log-like sleep. There is also a feeling of futility, perhaps you will never see these letters, if our release ever comes by way of repatriation, you certainly never will, for the Gendarmerie will never let a stack of letters through, if they refused even to pass a medicine label. If ever you do read these letters, long before you get this far, you will realize that monotony is the keynote of our existence here. No direct brutality, so far no bayoneting and torture and raping and all such accompaniments one had imagined as part and parcel of internment by an oriental nation, but just monotony, discomfort, dirt and overcrowding, and a futile kind of

94

busyness that nearly exhausts you, and which barely keeps you above the plimsoll line of cleanliness and decency.

Of course I can also sketch you some more Vignettes — they never fail to make me chuckle, even when feeling at my most irritable or discouraged. Here are several:

1. The vision of staid taipans of former days, stalking majestically to their respective washrooms, each bearing as company, Jeremiah Esq.

2. One of Shanghai's best known professional beggars of former days also, now on an equal financial footing with the rest of us, on the Comfort Fund basis, sitting back with a satisfied smile, having just heard the auctioneer's hammer fall to his bid of $850 for a box of cigars.

3. Two superb fights that took place in our hut, when our little K. of denture fame, and her next door neighbour came to blows following an exchange of views on the subject of snoring. K. rushed in, arms flying, and then remembered that she had just come off police duty, and still had on her armband, so she quickly removed it, so as to make the fight strictly legal, and in no way prejudicial to her dignity as a keeper of the peace. The next day, more views having been exchanged on the subject of snoring, with additional interchanges about the infringement by two inches of the frontier line between their two beds, the same two worked up another fight. This time, the dirty old floor mop came into play but K., remembering that her opponent still had on her *pince nez*, gracefully bent forward and removed them gently, saying the while "I am a lady . . ." and then she set to with the mop in her enemy's face. And really it was a very thoughtful gesture, seeing that *pince nez* would be irreplacable if once broken.

Personal irritations and feuds, and dissension in our Council are all symptoms of prison weariness and heartsickness. So they ought not to be taken seriously.

I have been fortunate in being able to contrive a cubicle to myself and the cats, whose charming and silent company I appreciate more and more each day. Do you suppose the Lord brought me to an internment camp that I might learn to admire cats, and cockscombs (do you remember how old Ah Yue would plant those wretched flowers in my Hungjao garden, no matter what I threatened, and now I almost like them!), not to mention, cooking, and chatties and curtains. In fact, I love my love with a C.

The eastern boundary of the cubicle is formed by a barrier of the dormitory's wardrobe trunks, and the northern is screened by a bamboo pole (acquired), and an upright (inherited), tied to the bed, and my rug and yards of unbleached calico are hung on the pole, and so I am curtained from view. Owing to the heavy preponderance of this Chinese calico, the ribald ones have christened my corner The Happy Valley Funeral Parlour. All I can retort is that the Senior Mourner, Cats and Custodian[32] (please note that this title is not to be confused with Guardian, as mentioned in my last letter to you!) all adore the privacy and freedom from draughts, and the comparative warmth.

DECEMBER 23RD. I see that my last words in my last letter were "comparative warmth." Had I but known what I was writing about, I ought to have said, genial heat. For, in the light of later events, I now call 52 degrees warm, I even fling my window wide open when that temperature is reached.

The first real cold came without any warning on December 1st, and caught us unprepared (as well it might, seeing that one is accustomed in Shanghai to having reasonably warm sunny weather until after Christmas) in even those things that we could do something about. Camp conditions in general had prepared us for the fact that though the stoves might be erected, we should rarely, if ever, have enough coal this year to light them as we did when we first came into camp. The draughts whistled through the floors, through the cracks in the wooden walls, only one plank thick, anyhow, and through the warped window frames.

For sheer numbed misery, I have never known the equal of those days. We crept out of bed, temperature 29 degrees, into the washroom, just as cold, and equally smelly as in the height of summer, cold trips for meals, for drinking water, and for me as schoolmarm, cold hours trying to teach, and the children trying to concentrate when they were frozen to the marrow, with frostbitten hands and feet, back to the cold hut, where I would creep into bed, fully dressed at all hours, with the two cats[33] as consolation and living hot water

---

[32] "The Custodian" — a male friend who did little services such as carrying and the like. He was nicknamed "the Custodian" by the teen-age young who also lived in the hut.

[33] Two kittens of the earlier litter went to other huts to cope with the rats. The kittens came from a family of proven ratters.

bottles. In two days hands and feet were ablaze with chilblains, and I anxiously awaited their appearance on nose and ears.

So we set to work stuffing up all the cracks, anointing our chilblains and reorganizing our personal habits. I realized that the nearer one could mould one's clothing and mode of life to that of a Chinese peasant, the better one would be able to face the cold. All fastidiousness as to washing, undressing at night, and such like had best be discarded for the time being, and I have found that it works beautifully. And though I hope that I never have to live in this manner again, I must say I have never suffered less from the cold, whilst living in unbelievably trying conditions.

I never change my underclothes, unless there is a gleam of sunshine lighting up my corner. And except that the topmost layer of fur jacket is exchanged for a padded dressing gown, I wear the same garments night and day. And as it is sometimes even colder in the hut than outside, we wear the same clothes indoors and out. But how many layers? Thick knitted vest and pants, woollen combinations, angora sweater, woollen ditto, flannel blouse, pyjama under slacks, long cotton stockings, woollen socks with gaiters on top, leather waistcoat, and either a padded jacket or fur jacket, head tied up in a scarf. It is tiring and tiresome to be so bundled up, I am just like a Chinese baby, if I fell down, I'd certainly need someone to help me up, being so padded out.

I also notice a curious bodily adaptation, where formerly I could put feet and hands, or rinse my head in very hot water, and loved it, now when I go near water, I can only stand a very moderate temperature, and these even during the relatively milder weather we are now having.

So, as the winter has got to be faced, I can deal with it, breathing a prayer for bigger and better curtains, both to keep off draughts and as a psychological defence against the floods of arguments, feelings, tears, squabbles and other outpourings of fifty-two cold and imprisoned females.

The camp has been through a pretty lean time of late, in the way of official rations, and because the British government have jibbed at the Comfort Money being docked at the rate of $200 monthly for hospital expenses, with only Japanese doctors on the panel, so for the time being, all Comfort payments have been stopped. So for the past six weeks there have been no laundry, no gate purchases, so eggs, honey and extra vegetables have been cut off our diet. The coal ration has been decreased, and this month's supply

arrived as practically the last shovel was being used up — so
ere will be barely enough for the kitchens and hot water sta-
(drinking water only) community stoves are forbidden. No
: hot water for washing, no hot showers and the Canteen is
dating itself.

DECEMBER 24TH. I must add a postscript to the above. That was
the situation yesterday. Today miracles are happening, or are
they Christmas treats? We have been told to register for laundry
again, we received rations of flour, raisins and sugar, and eggs were
on sale. And $200 per head of the sequestrated Comfort Money has
been credited to our accounts. And we had hot showers today. And
we were each allowed to send a free radio message to the outside
world. I do so wonder if you will ever get mine.[34]

And aside from miracles, school broke up, and I have two weeks
holiday and there are masses of festivities being prepared, all master-
pieces of building with strawless bricks. In fact, this Christmas will
be Christmas in spite of everything.

But in case you should think that I am a cheerful ray of sunshine, I wish you could see what I have grown to look like — or
perhaps I am glad that you can't see me. General appearance certainly qualifies me for endearing nickname coined by my fellow
lunatics "Lady Grape of Wrath." Further accentuated by flat feet
and fallen arches (apparently), straight hair, perm now being quite
extinct, and worst of all, a weight increase of twenty-six pounds. In
short, looks, charm, manners, brains, figure, deportment and memory have all gone — so how can I be anything else but depressed,
especially when I see to what state of raggedness my wardrobe is
now reduced?

JANUARY 3RD, 1944. To make a festivity out of a duty, we three,
monitor and two stooges, arranged to have a sandwich and ginger
wine party to see in the New Year, whilst sitting up to take the 1:30
a.m. roll call. The whole camp had been allowed the three hour
extension because of it being New Year's Eve, so a fancy dress dance

[34] Would Stanley Davys ever get my radio message? I had not heard from him
since 1941, when he had written to say that he was away from his New
Zealand home, on some sort of job in Australia to do with steel and the war
effort, rather hush-hush important. The only part of an address that I could
remember was "Broken Hill Mines" ... Australia. I felt rather a fool standing in front of the transmitter giving the name and "address?" of the person
to whom I would like to send a message.

was the highlight of entertainment for the young. We enjoyed our party, little dreaming of the drama that was about to be unfolded.

The drama concerned the one, whom for want of a better name, we have always referred to as "our problem child." I haven't hitherto told you anything about her, mainly because she defies classification. To begin with, to my way of thinking she is one of the most beautiful young women I have ever met. She must be in her early thirties, slim and boyish in build, with the most graceful, skimming, unearthbound walk I have ever seen. Short dark curly hair, fine features and violet eyes. And then she opens her mouth, and you hear the most appalling accent, with, as often as not, a flow of profanity to match. At the same time, she is quite one of the kindest souls here, I have never heard her, even in fun, say a harsh thing about anyone. About her past, she has a series of stories which, if a quarter of them were true, she would need to be sixty years old at least, in order to have had time to experience them. Rumours of all kinds have surrounded her ever since her arrival here — one of which is that she is a Japanese spy, quite unfounded, I have no doubt — all of which appeal to her *folie de grandeur*. I don't suppose you have any clearer pictures of her than at the beginning of this paragraph, so we'll just leave it at that. Well, we had seen her going off to the dance, looking a picture of loveliness — really breath-taking, in her Manchu gown. I remember thinking idly that she was putting on some weight around the hips. At 2 a.m. Muriel awoke to say that our Manchu lady had not returned, so she must go and report her absence to our Representative. We didn't take it very seriously, with true camp ribaldry, a very probable answer had suggested itself.

But by 9 a.m. it was proved that she and a couple of her young boy friends had escaped. She must have worn her riding breeches under the gown, hence the apparently fatter hips. The three of them had put in a short appearance at the dance, and then slipped away, getting a good start before the much deferred roll call.

All this morning has been spent with questioning by Authority, and their going through her pathetic belongings — when she wore her rags, they looked stunning. But without her vivid personality, they are just rags of the most soiled and tawdry nature. A soiled blue evening dress cut down into teddies, dirty mules with bedraggled wisps of ostrich feathers trimming. Her camp bed in such tatters that her legs lay along her suitcase underneath, and her shoulders were slung, hammock-wise, on the green corduroy pants which belonged to one of the darkie boy friends. Since Authority has departed from the hut, looking very wise, we have been waiting around, uneasily, wondering what further restrictions we shall inherit in the way of punishment.

This excitement has put out of mind, to some extent, the very lovely Christmas we spent. I could not have believed one could have had a happy Christmas in camp, and yet it was so. The day was sunny, and not too cold, so we all dressed up as well as we could, having regard to the state of our wardrobes, and according to what duties had to be performed. Those of us on school holidays, undertook kitchen, water or vegetable chores, to relieve the regular workers.

I loved the traditional side, which was heavily underlined. Carols, both at concerts, and on Christmas Eve the singers were pushed along on one of the Camp Service trucks, and they went singing from block to block, and hut to hut, simply delightful, and taking one back to childhood, as one drowsily listened to the music, sounding so clear and unearthly, in the still frosty atmosphere. We also had a reading of the Christmas Carol, the dining room was festooned with home made decorations of evergreens and berries. Presents, of touching ingenuity, were exchanged. Our Red Cross parcels arrived on the 24th, and the Swiss Community had remembered those who do not ordinarily get parcels. There were Santa Claus parties for the children — imagine the amount of time and effort needed to bake cakes for them all, and to produce a gift apiece.

I was just putting this letter away, when Muriel, our monitor, came in with the notice from the Commandant regarding our punishment for last night's escape. Excepting for one item, not nearly so severe as we had expected. Roll call in future to be at 9 p.m., and lights out at 9:30 instead of 10:30, and no one allowed out of billets before 7 a.m. — who would choose to be during this cold weather? And Carmelita and myself, as stooges to Muriel, rejoice at the early roll call — that last hour of sitting up in the cold, waiting to check in the inmates who had been out visiting was almost more than we could bear — loving our beds as we do. The bad item is that the whole New Territory is put out of bounds, including the school buildings, which is really catastrophic for the 300 children, who were just getting used to a more orderly school routine, and feeling the benefit (though they wouldn't know it!) of improved discipline. Now when the new term opens, we shall have to go back to our odd holes and corners, and things will slip back into the bad old ways.

BULLETIN ON THE CHILBLAINS BELONGING TO THE OLD LADIES OF B WEST.

Margery Warton (Carmelita)	Feet had convulsions during the night. Hut temperature 28 deg.
Peggy Pemberton-Carter	Feet and hands in a state of coma.
Irene Rayden	Disastrous condition due to surfeit of so-called remedies, including one which is alleged to be an old Cossack custom.
Kate	First virulent symptoms appearing.

JANUARY 16TH, 1944.   Cold! Cold! Cold! that is the monotonous tune that accompanies every action of stupid, numbed limbs. And as for thought, one's brain feels like a frozen sponge. Consequently tempers are short, and there are daily rows over lights, space, curtains, open windows, the time, loaned articles, jerries, and what have you; with a *passion*, in certain quarters, to "get to the bottom of the matter," as if the matter had any bottom, excepting coldness, boredom, and sick-to-deathness of the same faces, idiosyncracies and futile daily bustle that leads nowhere.

My co-stooge and I, by tacit agreement, retire to our beds whenever we hear raised voices. We find that if you just leave things alone, they solve themselves, as like as not. And I must say that I can still forget most things when I am behind my curtains, under cover with the cats.

Today we have been officially informed that the three escapers have been recaptured at a brothel in Yalu Road. Their story was that the girl and one of the lads left to get married, and the third lad tagged along to be the witness. This has provoked much laughter in our low neighbourhood. I suspect the truth is that her much-vaunted Buddhist passe-partout medal counted for less than nothing at the nearby temple, and in the end lack of food, money, clothing or plans drove them to Shanghai. We had all expected cleverness at least, from her — hairbreadth adventures and triumphant arrival in Chungking, with broadcasts on how she escaped from Lunghua.

Our daily existence is complicated still by the descent of deputations of Army, Consular and Legal Gentlemen, who come to our hut, to examine "X marks the spot," and each time it means hiding our chatties (behind the throne in one of the "horse-boxes," with a long suffering female sitting on guard) or if we have been able to scrounge enough wood and coal to light one of the hut stoves (both wood and coal have literally to be searched and scratched for, piece by piece) we have to hastily extinguish it, *lighted stoves being forbidden*. However, it helps to lend drama to life.

JANUARY 30TH. The dull routine received a rude shock last week, and the old dreads and uncertainties of pre-camp days descended upon us, when Eric Pollock was taken away to Bridge House for "questioning." Rumour has it that one of the escaping lads implicated him in the course of his "questioning."

The day after this shock, all inmates' baggage was searched, not too thoroughly, shall we put it that way? Maps, hot plates, foreign currency and any kind of tools were the objects in demand. Charles Rayden spent the time of the search in walking around the compound with his bucket on his arm, covered neatly with a towel. Anyone would have thought he was going for his shower — but all his knicknacks were in the bucket. And most of us had time to do something about our particular treasures. Personally I found that my canna bulb storage under the hut — was not in vain. And the general idea is that if our brains aren't at least one step ahead, we just deserve to lose whatever is being searched for. The actual fact of this search has proved a blow to the "rights" of those who are still unable to grasp that, name notwithstanding, we are prisoners in an internment camp, and that there is a war going on.

Last night, David Braidword's winding up of the lecture on Parliamentary Procedure, upon seeing a posse of Gendarmes entering and clanking round the dining room, was a masterpiece of witty aptness. "Ladies and Gentlemen, the last time the military invaded the House of Commons was upon that memorable occasion when Oliver Cromwell entered, and said, "Remove that bauble." The audience took the hint, laughed, and folded up their chairs and went back to their billets, to the evident bewilderment of the Gendarmes.

We all feel that the news must be excellent, because they are getting offensive and triumphant, with slappings whenever they feel like it.

And thinking back, how many curtailments and privations have been gradually forced upon us. No gate purchases, no Comfort Money, official rations of food and coal reduced, hot plates and irons confiscated, chatties and stoves only when they feel like giving permission for their use, boundary paths all out of bounds, and drastic rulings over lights — understandable with last month's bill $47,000, with a surcharge of $520,000 for over consumption.

By all we hear, prices in Shanghai are going in the same direction as Germany's at the end of the last war. Coal is $30,000 a ton, charcoal $17,000, and even a humble candle costs $50.

Today gendarmes from Shanghai came for Eric's baggage, and a rumour is circulating that he has been sentenced to eight years imprisonment in Ward Road gaol. A stiff sentence, but even at our most pessimistic we don't often believe that the war will last that long.

APRIL 5TH. I haven't written to you for over two months. The bitter coldness, making it difficult to hold a pencil even in mittened hands, has been largely responsible, and the endless monotony holds one in its grip for weeks on end. But today is an anniversary of sorts!

The most exciting thing that has happened to us during this past year, was the arrival at the end of last month, of our first Red Cross parcels from America. If I could only tell you or the Red Cross, how wonderful those parcels are, not only the food itself, but the beautiful way in which each item of food is packed, either in cellophane, or shining tin — all so suggestive of a great rich country, and so different to the shabby squalor of our lives. We each got one box containing milk, butter, jam, chocolate, corn beef, ham, sugar, soap, cigarettes, *and* coffee. The last item is the thing I love best of all. Quite literally, I can face anything, cold, hunger, tiredness, or exhausting heat, if I can have a good cup of coffee. Outside I always thought that coffee was a pleasant drink, but here it has the power to make even this existence more bearable. You can guess from this, that coffee has become my weakness. With others it is cigarettes. Inveterate smokers are in a state of near collapse the week before our monthly parcels are due, their supply of smokes having given out, they simply cannot work, think, or sleep. And it is positively shameful the way we casual or non-smokers (I include myself) trade on their craving. At that time of the month, you can get anything out of a heavy smoker for a packet of cigarettes — eggs, flour, sugar, jam, bacon, or what you will.

A side show to the arrival of the American parcels is the sudden growth of Exchange Boards outside each of the billets. Offered: 1 tin of coffee. Wanted: 3 packets of cigarettes, etc., etc. The state of the market, and prices now provide a welcome change of topic from eternal rumours. The former are discussed and quoted with as much fervour as formerly was given to Stock Exchange prices. These boards have taken the place of the auctions we used to have, for one thing, with cessation of the Comfort money, few people have any money in their bank accounts, and also, quite rightly, it is forbidden to sell or buy these American gifts.

Never was spring more welcome than this year, and human beings, I think, must be fundamentally optimistic. The deadening cold is already all but forgotten, and we begin to stretch ourselves, literally and figuratively speaking.

I have discovered that by sitting in the bricked drain outside my window, I am sheltered from all wind, and I can get enough warmth from the sun to warm me to my very bones — a heavenly life-giving sensation.

These past weeks I have been working quite hard at the patch outside my window. From lessons learned from last year's floods, I have raised it several inches, turfed a portion, and extended the flower beds to the other side of the path. And the greatest find was a climbing rose that Muriel dug up for me, somewhere amongst the New Territory ruins. I have planted and pruned it, and so hope to have roses hanging around my window this summer. Excited out of all proportion to know what colour the flowers will be.

The cat family now increased by the arrival of young Timmy, the nicest of them all. Poor Mandy produced him, to her great surprise, but not to ours, seeing that we had endured the discomforts of Catty love life going on under our beds. So, Mandy, being a young and modern mother, went out and chased butterflies within two hours of his birth. She neatly parked him at the foot of my bed, under the bed clothes, and left him to her own mother and me to rear him as we thought best.

The schoolmarm's career is as usual. The young gangsters of IIB have acquired the elements of discipline, as a result of my having perfected the art of roaring. Discipline probably acquired at the price of a lifelong hatred of the French language. We have been graciously allowed back in the New Territory, so may now consider ourselves pardoned for the New Year's Eve escapes. They were sentenced to two years for each of the lads and eighteen months for the girl.

Rumours are still the breath of our life, and the indefatigable optimists who asserted positively that we would be out of this place last October, Christmas, Chinese New Year, now proclaim enthusiastically that it will be at Easter, or June, or at the latest next October. I can see no basis for their prophecies. I'm afraid that there will be another winter with all its miseries. And by next year there will be even more drastically reduced rations of food, light, water and coal — all painfully inadequate now. But perhaps by that time our life will be enlivened by guerillas and air raids. The former are already in the vicinity to such an extent that the gendarmes, for the past few nights, have taken fright and refused to sleep in their quarters, but carted themselves and their families over to Hiyashi's office in the main building. And the last Red Cross truck, as well as bringing our parcels brought out Japanese soldiers, guns and ammunition.

As for the expected air raids, regulations are about to be issued, governing our conduct. A delightfully garbled pre-hearing of them suggests that we have to put on gumboots, seize our bedding and throw ourselves into the nearest ditch — the entrance to our hut has a permanent couple of inches of green slime, so the outlook is depressing.

Irene, our star wit at this end of the hut has spent a busy afternoon chalking up names for each of our garden plots outside our windows — a subtle psychological summary, in most cases, of the owners' character.

MON REPOS   GARDEN OF ALLAH   THE LORELEI
ROOKERY NOOK   THE CUCKOO'S NEST   MON ABRI   CHATTY SQUARE
DUTCH TREAT   BOULDER DAM   WILLOW COURT

Really we are becoming very childish, in a good and a bad sense. If petty irritations lead to quarrels, an issue of sugar or tea or garden produce creates a delightful flurry of excitement, in spite of the fact that there are always those who invariably complain that the method of distribution (and a new one is tried each time, in an effort to oblige!) is *unfair*.

Each week brings along some curtailment, either in rations, canteen or privileges, and the latest is the stoppage of all allowances paid to dependants outside. Today E. received a letter from her parents, who are still out, saying that but for friends they would be homeless and starving, having had no allowance since February. Our Commandant, reading this in the course of his censoring activities added the following pencilled postscript: "Don't worry, and don't come to see me about this."

Another favourite remark of his when pleas for improved conditions here are brought to his notice is: "It is only a matter of mental adjustment." There are times when I would dearly like to adjust him.

Here is a list of terms, from the Lunghua glossary, all of which I hope I never hear again, once I return to freedom:

Comestibles. Cubicles. Co-ordination. Containers. Dire Need. Nos. 1-300. Welfare Fund. Spreads.

MAY 1ST. My dream of life, when I get away from here, will be to get away somewhere where one can be alone and unencumbered by the endless petty chores that here keep one as uselessly busy as a caged squirrel on its little wheel.

Today is a school holiday (we won't mention the fifty odd exercises that have to be corrected by tomorrow. Nor will we speak of the organization required yesterday in the matter of fuel scrounging for the chatties so as to have time to write this today!). It is 11 a.m. Since 6:30 I have cleaned my house, fed the family (now lying, an inextricable muddle of three generations, on my bed), washed two sweaters, towels and pillowcases, my hair and hairbrush. Went to the butchers for some more cat food. Fetched my drinking water and cleaned my shoes. And I am lucky in my having kind Willie Way, my "Custodian," carry my bucket of washing water, or else that would have to be done too. And also in having my breakfast of three slices of toast — made by our indefatigable Charlie Rayden — also brought to me, and so saving a journey to the dining room for *congee*.[35] (Since giving up this morning poultice, weight has gone down eight pounds, with corresponding decrease in indigestion. So now that the knee has been manipulated back into place, by a fellow internee, an osteopath by profession, I am almost completely under control though nothing can be done about sagging chins, crepy[36] neck and graying hair — damn them!)

At 12:30 I shall go and fetch lunch for our corner, then there may be time for a short instalment of the desperately needed chronic wardrobe repairs. Then those school books. Then it will be time to get the chattie lighted and prepare for the carefully planned evening meal with the Custodian — an hour when we put on a slight semblance of life's graces, both as to manners, and conversation.

[35] *Congee* is a sort of sloppy gruel of boiled rice and water.
[36] The colour and texture of French Crêpe de Chine.

106

After supper, garden watering, eternal tidying up for the night, filling bucket in case the water pump gives out (which it does increasingly often), some Russian study (if the light isn't too bad) and pleasure in the quietness of a nearly deserted dormitory, if it is a night with bridge, lecture and dancing going on in the dining rooms. I am all for bigger, better and more frequent entertainments, so as to profit by corresponding quietness in the hut. By 9 o'clock I am exhausted, and then there is the labour of getting oneself slightly clean in a basin of water — one's bath should always be a time of relaxation — and then clambering under the net and hoping that someone else will put the light out when Muriel calls: "Lights out."

Last week the wives and relatives of the men imprisoned at Hai-phong Road (the "dangerous political prisoners" who have been there since November 5th, 1942) were allowed to visit their men there. I was terribly disappointed that John Green's powers of imagination or persuasion hadn't been equal to getting permission for me to visit him. But it is something to have had messages, and to know that he is as well as possible under such conditions.

It was very moving to see the wives all dressing themselves in their best, and making such a gallant show. And in the evening, when they got back, there were many sad hearts, reaction following the excitement of the day, and the tiring trip.

MAY 30TH. A week of excitement. Two attempted suicides, one of them in our hut, Russian, plus insomnia, plus love. With true camp callousness we grumbled audibly at the poor thing for disturbing our rest hour and for causing additional unnecessary work for an already overworked hospital staff.

And last Tuesday morning it was discovered that five men had escaped. Judging by official reticence on the subject we judge that they have reached safety by now — we hope so, as we shall be punished either way. So far we have been deprived of our chatties — ostensibly on account of official visits to "X marks the spot." The day-old renewed permission to use the boundary walks and New Territory for everyone to picnic in has been rescinded, and garbage coolies are banned.

As the New Territory is closed to us, school has once more come to an abrupt end, and all teachers are enjoying an indefinite holi-day. If it goes on too long, even my sluggish conscience will creak a bit. Meanwhile the comparative leisure has been a boon, I've repaired my sorely tried wardrobe, knitted, cleaned and reorganized my hole in the wall, read quite a lot, got on with the Russian, added to the flower patch, and tried to think, an increasingly difficult process the longer one stays here. I can't describe the blurred state of one's mind. And it is the same with memory — I find myself forgetting names that I know as well as I know my own, and soon my memories of you and all we have done and seen together will be so vague as to seem something that happened to someone else, or something that I read about long years ago — but no longer anything that really is part of my life.

JUNE 9TH. The news of the invasion came officially in yesterday's newspapers, though we had already had flurries of rumours on the subject, via our bamboo wireless. We are all sick with excitement and anxiety. It is the first break in our stupid, doldrummy existence. If it goes well — and it MUST go well, nothing else in the world matters. The paper, of course belittles it to the utmost degree, which I think may be a hopeful sign. Dare one hope that Europe will be cleared up this year?

If I had been told, a week ago, that I should no longer be school-marming, I couldn't have believed it. And yet, beginning from a casual remark, dropped by Irene Rayden, here I am as Quarter-master in the hospital kitchen. An interesting, heavy-ish job, with plenty of scope for initiative and ingenuity, and lots of daily variety. The hospital itself is a Chinese peasant farmer's house, primitive but spotlessly whitewashed and well run under almost impossible conditions.

The grandeur of my title conceals the fact that actually one is a glorified coolie with a bunch of keys, a pencil and scraps of paper, and that one requires the tact usually associated with the doyen of the diplomatic corps.

Long hours away from the hut, which is an agreeable change. I go on duty after morning roll call, 9:15, and duties officially cease after supper, between 6 and 6:30 p.m. But there are a couple of slack hours after the mid-day meal, when I can relax in My Office, if so grandiloquent a title can be given to the tiny room where I have to do my "figuring out" and my requisitioning of stores, and where I also have to stack the bags of cereals, rations of garden vegetables and any Red Cross supplies.

I enjoy wheedling the extra pound of rice, meat or vegetables, etc. from the various heads of Departments. But it is niggling to dole out oil, salt and sugar, literally by the spoonful to each shift of cooks. But there are days of drama, when we inherit either a goose or a rabbit from the farm, or a ration of pork from the piggery. I consider yesterday's distribution a perfect masterpiece; out of 28 lbs of meat and bone, served 68 patients and 12 staff, served liver for 7 young children, then liver and kidney for 22 breakfasts, and made a tin of liver paste, with soup for everyone's supper!

Incidentally, the Cat family has made it plain to me that I must hang on to this job for evermore — the scrapings from plates are such a great consideration.

We have just had the surprising news that all the remaining enemy nationals are to be interned. A new camp/sanatorium is to be opened on Lincoln Avenue. It will be a great upheaval for the old people, though also in some ways, a relief, once they can get used to the idea. There will be many reshuffles, here and in other camps, as relatives will try to get transfers to the new place.

JUNE 12TH. Irene and Charles Rayden have decided to move over to Lincoln Avenue Camp, so as to be with their parents. So today we had a farewell party in our broken down community stove shack — a delightful festivity, if the surroundings lacked elegance, the food was heavenly, appetites terrific, and conversation and gaiety simply sparkling. All very different to some of the oppressive farewell functions I have attended in other days!

A disgraceful point to be chalked up against our gaolers is that they have insisted that every single one of the old people, regardless of health or age, report personally at the Church House. No exemptions whatever. Those who were unable to walk, had to be taken on stretchers. Those who are considered too ill for camp life will be confined in the Hospital, whilst the relative who has up to now been caring for them, will be sent to camp. So this means many pitiful separations, and will probably cause many deaths amongst the very old. I don't think I have ever before been so choked with fury at the stupid, wanton cruelty of the Japanese. They make such a song and dance about their "Bushido" — polite and kind — my foot! You know, that "polite and kind" was inscribed on a scroll at Hamilton House, in the early days of the war, where we used to have to queue up for hours, waiting for passes, handing in declarations and being questioned until you were so tired, you didn't know or care whether you were dead or alive.

A delightful, if apochryphal, story, has just drifted in, to the effect that Hiyashi has just received a post card from Chungking from one member of the last escaping gang, Murray Kidd, which reads: "Arrived safely. Wish you were here."

Well, the shower bath enthusiasts have had their last warm showers, because the boilers are to be removed by the Japanese military to help boost Japan's war effort scrap metal collection.

AUGUST 18TH.　It has been a long and trying summer. It began at the end of June and has continued unbroken until the end of last week. Day after day of grilling sunshine, never a drop of rain, and nights of suffocation under the nets, with compulsory lights out at 9:30 p.m. And this summer we have not been allowed the respite of a couple of hours in the comparatively cool air on the roofs.

In the hospital kitchen, we have worked at temperatures ranging between 104 and 118 degrees Fahrenheit! So I feel I have qualified for the perks in the way of cat's chow, better cooking, and a few extra degrees of warmth next winter.

But as usual, work is the major salvation and consolation. On my holidays, after the essential private chores were done I had no energy left for anything except to lie on the bed, kill flies and "fan my life away," in company with Carmelita.

This last week there has been a brisk northeast breeze, "no typhoon so far, from which may the Lord deliver us," which has cooled things down, and now one can resume miracles of knitting with practically no wool, and patching some of one's rags with other rags against the winter — which soothsayers promise us will be long, severe and early. God help us.

My corner greatly improved both as to looks and comfort since I swung the bed West and East, along the window, instead of the usual North and South or vice versa. Now I am almost in the poplar trees, and watching their shimmering movement I can forget the squalor at my back. The garden patch is still a blaze of colour, in spite of the awful summer, and I have two melons just ready to cut! This consoles me for the major disappointment in the matter of the one and only rose that appeared on the carefully transplanted climbing bush — one morning the most charming little white bud started to unfold itself — in the pride of ownership I decided to leave it until it was fully opened, and then spend long and delighted hours considering whether to leave it flowering on the plant, or cut it and stand it in a mug on my shelf, and so enjoy every possible atom of its fragrance. It was swiftly decided for me by the fact that someone else removed it whilst I was away on duty at the Hospital.

The cats still beguile me more than anything else here. They know my days on duty, and during those hours, they hide themselves in the big flower beds and sleep until evening, then when their watches tell them that I should be coming home, they arrange themselves into an impressive procession, and come to meet me along the main path, me stumbling home on my poor broken arches and shoes full of holes, and their first question is always "What have you brought us for supper?"

And so we joggle along from day to day. I sometimes dare to hope that Germany may collapse before the winter, but out here I can see no end. Perhaps we are too close to see things in their proper proportions.

We get shabbier from week to week, and to combat it we contrive all manner of ingenious devices, so that our patron saint should be Heath Robinson, and our motto: "From practically no straw, quite passable bricks."

AUGUST 21ST. The weekend of excitement we were all looking forward to, because of the expected arrival after weeks of waiting, of the promised canteen supplies, as well as gate purchases of peaches, International Red Cross donations, our parcels and camp transfers, all of which promised a welcome break after our long spell of the doldrums, wherein major points of interest were how many potatoes "Puss in Boots" manages daily to conceal in her gumboots while on vegetable duty, or how to discourage an otherwise aimiable stoker from washing his coal-dusty feet in the sole enamel bucket I possess in the Hospital kitchen, turned out to be a horrible nightmare.

On Saturday morning, three more escapes were discovered, followed by the usual tense waiting and wondering "how will we be punished this time." We hadn't long to wait. Eleven punishments, worthy of a child in a bad temper were formulated by H.I.J.M.'s Consulate in Shanghai, and transmitted to us by the Commandant, who was beside himself with rage and mortification. The deprivations include: No newspaper — the worst of the lot at this stage of the war, we just live from day to day for it, and rejoice as each familiar name comes to the forefront. No canteen or library, no letters, chatties, concerts or entertainments, garbage coolies once more banned. All private books and gramaphone records to be turned in. Two meals a day, and all occupants (except a small skeleton staff for the essential services) to be confined to their huts or rooms until further notice. Occupants of the buildings will be graciously permitted to proceed along the passage to the toilets. Food and drinking water will be brought to the billets. Resentment increased all morning, with murmurings about protest meetings as a demonstration, etc., mostly fanned by women.

After the mid-day meal, a crowd of children were turned out to play on the football field. I, as usual, was lying on my bed, when suddenly I heard screams, roars, and the sounds of beating, hissing and booing. All the awful sounds of the mob, which make one realize how thin is the veneer of good manners and orderliness. I thought "they" had turned upon the children. But it was S. (the friend and next door neighbour of one of the escapers) who had been questioned for the past five hours by the gendarmes, who had broken away from his questioners, and was running across the field. Seeing two guards closing in, he hit them, then a third gendarme joined in the chase and caught him, whilst the other two held him down. No. 3 beat him until he streamed with blood from scalp wounds. The windows of all the buildings had been filled with horrified onlookers, who then poured out on to the field, the men at a strange, almost primeval crouching run, they all closed round the guards, who were pressed back to back, looking green with fear. If they had touched their revolvers they would certainly have been torn limb from limb. The crowd then rescued S. and took him to the doctors for attention. The guards were carried along to F. block by the furious crowd, where they were met by the Commandant, who was seized by his lapels by an angry woman, who shook him like a rat, and called him a B . . . , a brute and swine.

Meanwhile our Council and the Commandant had been having a meeting to see what compromise could be reached between the outrageous orders and "face saving." With admirable courage and persistence, our Representative, David Braidwood, kept demanding "But what am I to tell these people," each time the Japanese tried to close the meeting without any conclusions having been reached. Finally the Dean turned the temper of the angry crowd by repeating to them the "assurances, given as gentlemen, by our honourable gaolers that the six men involved in the questioning would not be removed from the camp, or if they were removed, an independant witness could accompany them to testify that there would be no ill-treatment." (It is noteworthy that both these promises were broken within six hours.)

In the end, the Commandant announced that the broadest interpretation that he could put upon his orders was that he would allow

women and children to circulate within their own blocks only. At
the same time the Council prepared a memorandum showing that a
single shift of the essential services included 490 people — so what?

Husbands and wives in separate billets, boy and girl friends
hastily divided their joint stocks of jam, spreads, soap, thermos
flasks, etc., and made tentative plans for the exchange of messages,
or arranging rendezvous, against prolonged separation.

Essential workers, e.g., me, as half of the Hospital Kitchen execu-
tive, went on duty, an eerie journey through the deserted camp.

Buoyed up by promises that a representative from the Swiss Consulate would arrive at the camp next day, another demonstration
was called off. But all who arrived were eight military policemen,
armed to the teeth.

At 8:30 that evening, we all betook ourselves (and I took the
Cats!) to the fictitious security of our mosquito nets, expecting Roll
Calls at any and every moment during the night. But all was peaceful in our hut, though the opposite one had seven gents armed with
swords and revolvers and tin hats clanking down their aisle some time
after midnight. And all night we listened to the yells and screams
of the Chinese in the neighbouring village, no doubt being given
the works. Whilst in the compound guards shouted and stamped
about.

This morning the whole camp, even the essential workers, armed
with their equally essential passes, was confined to billets until after
the All Clear whistle was blown, which was past ten o'clock. Consequently there was no water for washing, flushing or drinking, and
nothing to eat, aside from our own stores. We all heard the water
truck arrive from Shanghai; they will spread the news of something amiss when they get back to town, for the camp must present
a strange picture to them, utterly deserted at an hour when it is
usually already a hive of industry with shifts going on and coming
off duty.

About 9 o'clock, the six men were smuggled off, we fear to
Bridge House. This happened after the visit of some Personage, so
high, that Hiyashi nearly bowed himself head over heels, every time
he addressed him or was addressed. S's bed and every possession
was taken to the Commandant's house, and we are wondering
whether he will get ten years per hit per guard, whatever may
happen to the others.

A hard morning on duty, though it was a salvation really to be
able to escape from the "non-essential" females in the hut, some

of whom are "a-rarin'" for a job, for the first time in history, so as to be able to get out of the hut. With no rations brought in yesterday, tried to accomplish the impossible in the way of diets for the sick and sickly. Actually Doris and the cooks stayed with the in-patients, and two stokers and myself went from block to block, delivering food to the outpatients. We met guards, bristling with weapons, patrolling the compound, others asserting the supremacy of the Co-Prosperity Sphere by smashing up chatties and collecting wire, rakes, handsaws, etc., presumably the few remnants that escaped the last round-up. Evidently neither gardening nor repairs are to be considered essential services.

Drinking water (two dippers per head and no tea) was delivered to billets. Hot congee at 11 a.m. (the first camp meal since 5:30 yesterday afternoon) and stew will be delivered at 4 p.m.

I shall return to the Hospital in an hour, to prepare for "Famine Relief" again. Doris and I will have to double our shifts whilst this crisis lasts.

The greatest sufferers are the "non-essential" men, cooped up in their rooms, with no activity possible, to help to take their minds off brooding.

And so we are waiting and longing for war news, even the garbled stuff that we get in the local paper. I wonder if some of the rage over this incident isn't partly due to the war situation, and whether they aren't using it as a pretext for inflicting hardships upon us that they have had in mind for some time. The Japanese mind likes to have a righteous and official pretext for all its most outrageous performances.

AUGUST 24TH. The pro-demonstrationists have justified themselves by crying: "Because of us, they returned the men, unharmed within twenty-four hours." I can't help thinking that because of them, the men were taken. We hear that they had a mixed outing, ranging from the night spent at the Pétain Gendarmerie in a cell with Chinese, and being told that they would be shot at the least provocation, to separate interviews with A Very High Personage, name unknown, at the Japanese Consulate, followed by an excellent meal, attended by the same high personage and our Commandant. They were finally sent back here (excepting S.) in a truck, with guards armed with Tommy guns! A mild demonstration of welcome was quickly squelched when N., for some reason thought to be its sponsor, was marched off to the Guard House and made to stand for two hours.

Everyone is chafing under the enforced confinement, though mercifully the book punishment had been waived. Confined to billets means what it says so literally, that we are not even allowed to go to the washing lines, ten yards from our windows, so these same windows are now bristling with neat little bamboos, *à la chinoise*, thrust through the legs of our panties.

The last two nights have been difficult. At evening Roll Call, slaps and hits galore, for offences varying from having one's hair in curlers and covered with a turban, to failing to have a two-year-old child up, dressed and standing to be numbered — at 9:30 p.m., mark you. During the night we were twice awakened with the whistle and order for Roll Call. I trust that by our superficially indifferent demeanour we were able to deprive the guard of seventy-five per cent of his pleasure at getting us up at 2 and 3 o'clock in the morning.

We are told that neither the Commandant nor the Chief of Police are able to control the guards any longer, and the two of them locked themselves up in the office to prevent the underlings from seizing the firearms stored there and using them on us. We also hear that this lot of guards are being sent away tomorrow, to be replaced by others. Presumably as a farewell gesture, they have spent all this morning in burning down the summer houses and furniture belonging to G block.

AUGUST 25TH.   Today we, that is to say, blocks A, B, C, D, H, J, and the Assembly Hall, are declared forgiven insofar as being allowed to circulate freely. E and G blocks have yet to be pardoned.

S. has been sentenced to one month's imprisonment in Ward Road gaol for "defiance" though Hiyashi advised him to plead "fear." A surprisingly light sentence, and probably it is just as well for him to be out of sight until the present tension has passed.

Further cuts in our rations have just been announced; we are told that the same is happening in all camps. Meat, vegetables, rice, flour, oil and bread are all to be reduced by one third.

Yesterday we reached the nearest we have yet come to starvation diet. There was enough flour in camp to make one thin dough pancake — just flour and water, more or less baked — for each person's mid-day meal. There was nothing else. But today we are back again to two daily meals, still euphemistically called breakfast and tea, served at 11:45 a.m. and 4:45 p.m., as they will most likely be invariable, they might just as well be called congee and soup. Today in the hospital we were able to eke out some eggless pancakes to elongate the sparse menu. It was pathetic to see our potwasher's gratitude at getting two of them as bonus to his plate of congee. I have seen the same look on a beggar's face. Awful.

Our other commodity restrictions increase steadily, mainly owing to power cuts. The water is only turned on for ten minute periods, amounting in all to four and a half hours out of the twenty-four. The state and smell of the toilets, as a result, unimaginably ghastly. We can only store small quantities of water, owing to universal lack and decay of containers. Repairs are out of the question, as all tools have once more been confiscated. Presumably one escapes by means of soldering irons and the like! Which isn't to say that we haven't, most of us, contrived caches of great ingenuity, where we secrete our most particular treasures (I include these unposted letters to you under this heading) against the day when things loosen up again, or that blessed, but infinitely remote day when we can return to life again.

The loss of the newspaper is the first thing that I have found to be nearly unbearable; for the rest, one can accommodate oneself.

We are now only allowed seven lights in the whole hut, and those only between the hours of 7:45 and 9:30 p.m. And we are promised a winter with no lighting or heating at all. As long as they leave me my bed and my cats, all is not lost!

NOVEMBER 8TH. It is a long time since I have written anything to you. For the first time since coming to camp, I have been thoroughly under the weather. To the question so often asked in cheap ads: "Have you got Bad Legs?" I have to answer "Yes" for the past six weeks. The poor weary things just gave up, or gave out, with a non-infectious form of erysipelas. Sole cure appears to be rest and warmth and sulphathiazol. Excepting for being a burden on others for the means of life — fetching my meals and water, doing my washing and cleaning up my corner and asisting with the Cat family, I have adored the rest — well worth the discomfort of the disease. I have read a good deal, finished up knitting that would otherwise never have got done before winter, and valiantly tried to repair the wardrobe by joining together two rags and thereby producing a third.

I hope to get back to work again next week, a rest in camp is fine for a time, but enough is enough! Time has a way of dragging if there isn't the steady routine of a job to delude you into thinking that time is passing quickly.

Since I last wrote there have been several flurries upon the surface of our backwater existence, but whatever happens or whatever one hears from the irrepressible optimists, we are still here, and likely so to remain for many months to come — barring a miracle. My guess is still one year from now.

Our Commandant, Hiyashi, was demoted as a result of the August escapes (coming on top of the others) and the demonstration, and about two weeks ago his successor, Yamashita arrived. He appears to be a much more dignified, reserved man, and with his arrival we were declared as completely forgiven; and the last privileges (excepting the roofs for sitting and concerts) newspaper and entertainments were restored to us. But the threat was added that another escape would entail the temporary punishments being made permanent, plus the stopping of our Red Cross parcels, and either confiscating or puncturing all our private stocks of tinned food.

Yesterday we had an echo of the whole affair, when S.'s belongings were piled on to a truck and driven away. We hear that he has finished his gaol sentence and is now being sent to another of the Civil Assembly Centres. And talking of sentences, we hear that John Wooley has escaped for the second time from Ward Road, this time successfully, and that $100,000 is being offered for his recapture.

The new Commandant has ordered, as a preventative against further escapes, that all unattached men between the ages of sixteen and sixty are to be billeted in B block, and that an inner fence of barbed wire is to be erected, making an easier perimeter for the gendarmes to guard. A reasonable enough order, from the Japanese point of view, but once the order came into the hands of the Council and the Billeting Office, caused more talk and upheaval than all the war during its five years! I have a shrewd idea that a good deal of the upheaval, and consequent stalling, is a species of delaying tactics. A wonderful game that can be played with our gaolers to an almost unlimited extent. Of course the order will have to be obeyed sometime, and I must say I have qualms of uneasiness about all the able-bodied men being herded together in one block — the Japanese now have them concentrated in one spot and can do anything they like with them. My dread is that if bombings become heavy in Japan they may be taken off to those areas as hostages.

Last month brought yet another cut in electricity, and, with the days beginning to draw in, we already spend some time groping in half darkness. No lights at all allowed in the early mornings, and at night, one light is allowed in the Washroom only, from 7 p.m., and six lights for the whole hut from 7:15 to 9 p.m. As this does not permit any of us being able to see to read or play bridge or sew, we have been trying out a scheme for different sections of the hut to have the whole six lights on different nights. As to the fair parcelling out of them, we get great and glorious exhibitions of "Community Spirit" and "Your Duty Towards Your Neighbour." The middle of the hut thinks it is a fine arrangement that leaves the ends in darkness, but not so funny when it is their turn to sit in a blaze of darkness and vice versa! Our end is always philosophical, due partly to Carmelita and myself being ever ready to lie down, if not sleep.

Roll call is now at 8 p.m., at which we have to stand fully dressed, according to the volatile fancies of whichever guard happens to be on duty. For instance some of them decline to allow head bands, others get enraged at day pyjamas, or overcoats, or anything suggestive of a dressing gown or slippers. This is the only thing that prevents the two ex-stooges (now resigned from Assistant Monitorships) from going to bed peacefully at sunset.

A pathetic example of the state of mind to which we have come, is our pitiful excitement at permission having been given for us to extend our billet space by four inches — yes, inches! into the centre aisle. So now the grand total area for each person, with their bed and trunks is nine feet four inches by four feet!!! But our greatest excitement has been the release of thirty-odd neutral born, but British passported, women. This gives the irrepressible optimists the excuse to assert that we'll all be out before Christmas, or the New Year, or the end of January, or February.

In spite of laughter from these same optimists, I have been busy preparing my pocket handkerchief garden for the spring by collecting wild violet roots and planting them in clumps, sowing wallflowers, forget-me-nots and snapdragons and training the climbing rose around the window. So I shall now repose myself for the winter — which looms ahead of us, bleaker even than last year, with little lighting, no heating or hot water and reduced rations.

I can almost bear the prospect when I read anything so delicious as the following heading from the *Shanghai Times*: "Successful Concert Given Under Auspices of Anglo-American Joint Fleet Annihilation Celebration Society."

NOVEMBER 12TH.   Yesterday morning, Armistice Day, we had our first thrilling moment, since coming into camp — or rather, since December 1941. At exactly 9 a.m. as the guard entered our hut for morning Roll Call, there was a run of terrific explosions, and we knew at once that it must be an Allied air raid, so long waited for, and so greatly longed for. We all played our parts well in the comedy, the guard walking past us, with impassive face, and ourselves mechanically calling out our numbers. But the suppressed excitement, after all these years of dull monotony, was almost more than one could bear. After the guard left the hut, our excitement broke loose, and we all shouted and cheered, and hung out of the windows, trying in vain, to catch a glimpse of the planes. Later in the day, a mildly worded Proclamation appeared, in which we were told to refrain from any demonstrations of joy during future raids, and equally to refrain from leaning out of the windows. I feel that *They* must be slipping — in the good (or bad) old days, the least they would have threatened would have been "Off With Your Heads."

And I must add, that cautious minded as I am when it comes to believing good news, there are days when the communiques we get via bamboo methods are all confirmed in the paper. We read of a landing in the Philippines, naval action around Formosa, and consolidation in France, Belgium and Holland.

From Shanghai we hear that Japanese occupation C.R.B. dollars are collapsing from day to day. The latest sterling rate is $4,000 to £1. Coffee $4,000 per lb. Rice $22,000 per picul. A taxi to Shanghai and back here, $22,000. Coal $120,000 a ton.

We worked out than an average monthly parcel must cost our contacts between $10,000 and $20,000. And to think that when I came here I left Y. $10,000 to spend on fresh food for me, and we calculated it as a generous estimate for one year. Indeed, I almost lay awake at nights thinking I'd been wildly extravagant in allowing so much.

Here at the newly re-opened Canteen, when they come in, we unblinkingly pay $28 for an egg, $490 a lb for sweets, $300 a lb for uneatable jam, $300 a lb for lard, $210 a lb for peanut butter and $240 a lb for sugar. And the next consignment will have left these prices far behind. Well, we can't have Co-prosperity in Greater East Asia without paying for it.

MARCH 21ST, 1945. The grim and so much dreaded prospect of our second winter here more than fulfilled itself. My mind is just a blur as to what really happened from the end of November until now; a frozen, stupefying blanket numbed all my faculties — and everybody else's too. I thought our first winter here was about all anyone could bear, but this one places that one under the heading of temperate weather. According to official figures, it is the longest and coldest ever recorded in the Shanghai area, with 79 days of unbroken freezing and below freezing temperatures. I remember that on the morning of Dec. 1st we woke up to a temperature of 28 degrees F. with a strong northwest gale blowing, after which, for four and a half months we hardly ever looked up again, but constantly slipped down to lower levels; 18 degrees F. was the hut's best effort, with an outdoor temperature of 17.

Chilblains, frostbite, septic hands and feet and sores and cuts that couldn't heal because of the cold were all accepted as inevitable. The Cat family, by sleeping in bed with me, saved me from the former miseries. Which brings me to the saddest days I have spent here. A month ago, the food situation became so acute, murmurs in the hut became louder and more frequent over the catty serenades, that I miserably agreed to have the two ladies sent to wherever all good cats go, it being one of the last chances to have it done humanely, one of my camp friends having still a couple of ampoules of morphine. I still have young Timmy to console and beguile me with his miniature wildcat ways, and even feeding him takes all one's ingenuity!

After much stalling and passive resistance, the inner barbed wire fence was finally erected by Chinese coolies. And incidentally we thereby replenished our sadly depleted stocks of chattie firewood, as a brisk trade was done with them for sawn-off lengths of the fence poles. The current rate being half a pole for one loaf of bread. So now the clutter under my bed is more complex than ever, with poles rolling about and getting in the way when one is looking for the frying pan, or the odd sock, or pencil, because it is an odd thing, but every single article that I lose, always finds its way to the remotest corner under my bed.

120

At Christmas the Swiss Consulate and our private contacts were unbelievably generous in sending in parcels of fresh foodstuffs, and bulk supplies of meat, cereals and vegetables, so for that week we lived really well. The notable celebration in our hut was provided by Carmelita and myself offering to prepare plum puddings from donated supplies from any of our inhabitants who were alone and unlikely to receive puddings from outside. We thought that about ten might come forward with their individual contributions of either an egg, a handful of dried dates, a spoonful of flour or lard, etc. To our amazement, forty wished to join in, and offerings poured into my cubicle, and Carmelita and I set to work to make these remarkable puddings. Can you picture the cold sticky misery of picking and cutting fruit, one's mittened paws hardly able to hold a knife or a raisin. However, everything went in, carrots, sweet potatoes, tinned fruits, dates, raisins, jam and honey, a very little sugar, lard, the kernals of prune stones, stewed huckleberries, bread and flour, some hoarded spices. Being in a Favoured Position, I was able to get two of the puddings cooked, and Babbie supervised the cooking of the other two, and the result was what seems to me the heavenliest pudding I have ever eaten. Each one weighed around eight pounds — so you can imagine the helpings were hearty, none of your delicate slices that one nibbles at, after having been already overstuffed with a plate of turkey, ham and trimmings. At our end, we elected to eat just plum pudding, in the evening, just before bedtime. And the well-filled, well-anchored sensation was just delightful, and we all slept the sleep of children. No nonsense about lying heavy on the stomach.

After this burst of high living, we returned to our life of steadily diminishing everything. Days without bread, days with no meat, or no vegetables. Sugar has disappeared from the official rations, and we badly miss the odd two ounces per head that we used to receive from time to time. But we do get a tablespoon of egg flakes once a week — and they are invaluable. For the rest, restricted or no water, ditto coal, restricted lights, toilets that are chronically blocked and that can only be persuaded to gurgle feebly by churning round with a mop — the mop wears out and we can barely find rags enough to make another. No more Canteen, and practically nothing left to talk about, excepting quarrels and rumours until just lately, when even the newspaper admissions are so cheering that even I begin to dare to hope that we may soon unhook our harps from Babylon's willow trees! It will be time — for you have no idea of our poverty, you see I have to write in pencil, have to save the last dregs of ink to address envelopes when I write locally on the Red Cross forms. Safety pins, cottons, needles and elastic are all commodities for which you can obtain almost anything in exchange.

MARCH 1945. Just after Christmas I received a Red Cross letter (regulation 30 words including address, printed only!) from T. S. Yieh, telling me that the Japanese Authorities would no longer allow Chinese nationals to send Red Cross parcels to Enemy Nationals. So I concluded that this was the beginning of a period of near starvation.

I should have known T.S.'s faithfulness and inventiveness better. In January my usual parcel arrived — sent by a Mr. Oliveira. In February it came from a Mrs. Alvarez, Portuguese and Spanish nationals.

APRIL 1ST. Today is Easter Sunday, glorious weather, sunny and warm, and the birds are singing, and at last things are growing after the terrible winter. I am writing to you out of doors, from the vantage point of what we call Guttersniping. It really means that I am sitting right in the brick drain that runs along the hut, with my back to the hut itself, sheltered from all wind, and revelling in the sun. Layers and layers of clothes have been discarded, and it is grand to be able to move one's limbs again, instead of just shambling along, a bundle of frozen misery.

We are also well fed again. A couple of weeks ago, we each received four Red Cross parcels, either three American parcels and one British, or else four Americans. I can't tell you the difference it makes to have coffee again, and sweet puddings and prunes and chocolate and butter and cheese.

And even more thrilling than the parcels, we have, from time to time, actually seen the Allied planes flying over — we have heard bombings somewhere in the direction of Woosung quite often, but to actually see the planes, makes all the difference.

From Shanghai we hear of the crazily mounting prices. C.R.B. dollars are now 5,000 for one U.S. Dollar, and coal is half a million dollars a ton if you can get it. $2,000 for a chicken, and in my last local parcel I received 14 ozs of fruit cake with the bill attached, namely $2,170!

We also hear that the Japanese are turning out all tenants, regardless of nationality from the big apartment houses — military necessity, they say. My guess is that they will use them as block houses, regular fortresses, should the Allies land here. Meanwhile the French are going through a bad time since the Japanese coup in Indochina, and we hear of 22 families literally on the streets, homeless and jobless, until some sort of relief can be arranged.

And talking of relief — I am a walking fashion plate of Dire Need clothes. This delightful term originated in a letter our Council sent to the Swiss Consulate, pointing out that so many of us were in dire need of shoes, clothes of all kinds, and could they help? Eventually bales of corduroy slacks, gaudy check flannelette blouses, towelling socks, and rather half-witted looking shoes and sandals arrived, and now we go around looking like nine hundred pairs of twins, but feeling quite set up — myself especially when I remember that I have signed an I.O.U. to the British government, through the Swiss Consulate, for $30,000, being the price of one check blouse and a delightfully roomy pair of shoes, even if I do have difficulty in deciding which foot is which, or which is the heel and which the toe.

APRIL 3RD. Yesterday we had our first real air raid over the Lung-hua area. American planes swooping so low that we could see every marking, and even the crews, shrapnel flying around and falling on our roof, bombs dropping and huge fires started at Lunghua aerodrome, the cement works and Hungjao aerodrome. Can you imagine our excitement to *see* something really happening at last. Official instructions were that we should shelter under our beds, but as everybody's Under Bed Area is as full of essential rubbish as mine, this instruction is not so helpful. So I assumed my favourite position On The Bed, and a few others squatted under the cement troughs in the washroom, amongst the buckets and gumboots. The rest hung out of their windows, until growled at too threateningly by the gendarme, one of whom was posted at each billet to prevent people from going outside.

MAY 7TH. Somewhere about this season our farmers (the "farm" was another Chinese peasant building next door to the Hospital, and opposite to the Japanese Commandant's ugly red brick bunga-low) Liza Andrews and "Nobby" Clark informed our British Camp Representative that the time was approaching when Gloria, our only cow, would be needing a bull, if the supply of milk for the hospital, the children (about 300 of them!) and the aged was to be maintained. Our B.C.R.[37] promised to take the matter up with

37 British Camp Representative.

123

our Japanese Commandant, who was most sympathetic, but would have to refer to his seniors, as the nearest suitable bull lived at Culty's Dairy in Shanghai's French Concession (several miles away, much of the distance across country, by footpaths until the main roads were reached). As the bull could not be walked to Lunghua, Gloria, accompanied by a suitable escort, escorted by an armed escort, would have to walk to Shanghai early one morning, and in due course walk back to Lunghua, and above all be back in time for evening roll call. Eventually permission was granted, and the number of volunteers for escort was phenomenal, and one fine morning, Gloria was led forth, with her civil escort, escorted by their military escort armed to the teeth (swords and revolvers). The big Lunghua gates were flung open, and, to the applause of several hundred of us, the bridal procession set off — I cannot say at a brisk trot, because cows don't trot — perhaps a "brisk amble" gives an idea of the tempo?

I would like to be able to add that the bride wore a wreath around her horns — in my imagination it all suggested an ancient pagan, fertility rite.

The actualities were these: footsore and weary, cow and escorts eventually arrived at Culty's Dairy, which at this time was being managed by friends of so many of us old timers: Boris and Billie Krenov. Boris was a charming, witty, pre-Soviet Russian, who, before 1918, was a manager of the Russo-Asiatic Bank in Shanghai. Billie, his wife, was a delightful Shanghai girl (American mother, Scottish father — Barney Firth) and much loved by all. Boris decided, that in order to keep Billie out of internment, he would take out Soviet papers — so their own home and the Culty Dairy, at this time were 100% neutral. Over the months and years, with the collapsing currency, they (in theory, wisely) invested their spare cash in food — mostly vodka — the theory was certainly correct. But in practice, every friend, from every camp in and around Shanghai, having wangled a medical or dental appointment (perfectly legitimate) for treatment beyond that available within the camps, were able to "stop over," with their escort guards, for a short visit at the Krenovs who, with Russian/American hospitality, saw that their guests departed neither hungry nor thirsty. So, as a hedge against inflation, or the collapsing currency, the garage full of cases of vodka was not a success.

Back to the "Wedding Breakfast." Hungry civil escort *and* their equally hungry military escort, enthusiastically accepted Billie and

Boris' invitation to lunch — and what would they like to drink? The military escort, still relatively full of authority, replied "alcohol not allowed." "Ah," said Boris, "what about some milk? The quality of Culty's milk is well known." Agreed. So Boris diluted the milk with his stored vodka (or would it be vodka diluted with milk?) it was pronounced "excellent." After another round or two — swords were discarded — and revolvers. Tunics unbuttoned. Both sets of escorts slept blissfully. Around sunset, they aroused themselves — for after all Gloria had to be walked home. I cannot describe the journey home, but I do know that the whole "wedding party" arrived back at Lunghua, after dark, in a state of blissful mutual affection — arms flung across each other's shoulders — with songs — swords trailing — and perhaps, after all, Gloria's horns were wreathed with flowers?

No newspapers for the last two days. But the food cart, and other sources, have brought us the news that Germany has at last capitulated; the news of the past week has pointed to this being on the point of happening, and now we really can allow ourselves to believe in the indescribable lightening of one's heart. I had imagined that one would believe and rejoice at the same moment, but there have been so many false rumours, dribbles of true news, and above all, we are still here — so one has to get used to a slow spring after a long winter.

Well, the two most malign influences have gone — Hitler and Mussolini, (it is odd, with what malicious delight the Japanese are now belittling their former partners) and one of the benign influences. Roosevelt's death was announced to us by an official bulletin. What tragic irony that he couldn't live to see the completion of his work. We were allowed to hold a memorial service for him, providing we didn't mention the fact in either our local or overseas Red Cross letters. The two minutes silence was the most complete silence imaginable, all the more moving because one of the characteristics of camp life is incessant noise during all the waking hours.

Now dare one hope that six months more will see the end out here? It only took eleven months, to the day, for Europe to collapse after the opening of the Second Front.

Seeing that the only way we can celebrate anything outstanding is by having something special to eat, this evening I opened one of my two tins of Delmonte fruit salad, so jealously guarded for just this occasion. The second is to be opened on the day Japan gives up, if we are still here and alive to tell the tale. Rumours are very persistent that we are to be moved inland somewhere, and are only to be allowed to take hand baggage which we can ourselves carry. No beds, bedding or stores, which will suggest a winter of unbelievable wretchedness if we are still interned at that time. An alternative, and more unpleasing rumour, is that we shall all be shot the moment the Allies land. So take your choice. But meanwhile, the fruit salad was delicious beyond all belief, and the chosen company was very appreciative of Mr. Delmonte's canning skill.

MAY 31ST.   I am too restless to write more than a few lines at a time to you. As I had always imagined, these weeks since Germany's collapse are the hardest (psychologically speaking) that we have had to live through. So much movement and changes for the better in Europe, and our life here is as usual, with still further decreases in rations, which have now reached their lowest level — so far! No breakfast on four days a week, except for a ladle of green tea, and on the other three days, 1 oz of congee. Today's mid-day meal consisted of 1 ladle of watery cabbage soup with a few strings of tripe in it, 1 oz of potatoes and 2 ozs of beetroot. And we do not have an evening meal. The bread ration has been increased from 12 ozs to 1 lb daily, but since the increase it has become quite uneatable, heavy and sour and mouldy. (We do find that if you cut it into squares and dry it in the sun, it makes quite good chattie fuel!) It was very opportune that the Swiss Consul, Emil Fontanelle, visited us today, and was genuinely horrified when he was shown the bulletin posted up, which gave our daily official ration and the number of calories, 300! He left with promises to do everything possible to have bulk supplies sent in to us. To be fair, I don't think the Japanese are deliberately set on starving us, though I don't suppose they'd mind if we do, but they just can't get either supplies or transport from the Chinese, who can now see which way the wind is blowing, and are acting accordingly.

I have been on three week's sick leave from the hospital kitchen. The *bad legs* again — blast them! At their best and blotchiest, I can compete with any Chinese beggar sitting on the pavements, I only need some dirty red plasters to stick on the sore places.

The best things in life at present, are the heavenly weather and my flower patch outside the window — lovely, as I lie here on the bed resting *the legs*. As I had hoped, the white rose is a picture, framing my window in a perfect wreath, and looking beautiful at all hours, whether sunlit or moonlit. And of course there is always my Timoschenko to enliven proceedings — even when he forgets to conduct himself as a cat and a gentleman should.

JUNE 17TH. The Swiss Consul was as good as his word, and through him, the I.R.C.[38] are doing valiantly in sending in supplies, against heavy odds of Japanese officialdom and a currency gone to glory. Official prices this week are: Beef and bacon, $3,000 a lb. Pork $6,000 and vegetables $1,000 per lb. Rice $6,000,000 a zah. And we paid $420 an egg without blinking. For a few days bread was de-controlled from its price of $700 a loaf, and black market prices rocketed to $5,000 a loaf. But the Soviets, as ever, were able to exert their usual successful pressure, and it is now being sold at its controlled price again.

The most disquieting rumour that we have had lately is that the men in Haiphong Road are to be moved up north very soon. A horrible thought, for heaven only knows what will happen to them once they are so far away from all communications. I fear that it is only a step on their journey to Japan, where they will be posted at all the most heavily bombed spots. This general change around is part of the Japanese policy at the moment. Already two of the Civil Assembly Centres in Shanghai have been moved; they have gone down to the old Sacred Heart Hospital in Yangtzepoo. We hear that the conditions of life and the state of the building are indescribable. Rumours of our own removal are once more very persistent; so can only hope that something drastic will happen before they have time to get us started on our journey.

AUGUST 11TH. We are seething with excitement since the news of Russia having declared war against our little gaolers. This is the third dramatic surprise she has sprung upon us since 1939. It was officially announced to us yesterday, but we all "knew" it the day before — the bamboo wireless being up to standard! This is one of the odd things I shall always remember about imprisonment — the impossibility of keeping news out. I suppose human curiosity on the one hand and the love of imparting information on the other account for the fact, and make it rank with the primitive requirements of sleep, food and warmth. When the bulletin came out, we were requested to make no demonstration, but as you can imagine, we are so excited and thrilled, we can none of us settle down to anything. This must bring the end so much nearer — maybe only a

38 International Red Cross.

127

matter of weeks now. It will solve the Manchurian army problem, the only remaining great obstacle to peace, for we gather that the rest are ready enough.

C.R.B. currency has taken another downward plunge. Bread is now $3,700 a lb. One box of matches $10,000. Soleing and heeling shoes, $100,000. And in the canteen last week we paid $1,200 for two eggs each.

Actually we are living very well these days, the Swiss supplies are coming in regularly, so as well as the Japanese rations (which, oddly enough, have also improved) we have received rolled oats, cracked wheat, potatoes, tomatoes, onions, sugar, lard, eggs, peanut butter, jam, honey, maltose, bicarbonate of soda, meat, pepper and curry powder. I find that the improved diet is already showing results *chez moi*. Less starchy foods have reduced the awful weight down to 134 lbs, and done away with the tired heaviness. And a new treatment of vaccination seems to have put an end to the swollen lips and bad legs.

LATER.   Of all the ten thousand different ways I had pictured hearing the news of the end of the war, I never dreamed of the actual one! Just as I had written the last sentence above, some of the young girls of the hut rushed in shouting and laughing — "The war is over! The war is over!" And then miraculously one heard the same cry echoing from the whole camp. And yet if you asked how they knew, or who had told them, nobody could say. They just heard someone calling the news, so they took up the cry. My first reaction: "I don't believe it." And yet — it *could* be true.

AUGUST 12TH. EVENING.   If anyone had told us, a week ago, that this Sunday we should be celebrating peace and victory, we would have cried out "Crazy," and yet that is what we have been doing today, in a daze of happiness. Naturally, the only way we ever celebrate is by eating something special. So I, as the experienced Quartermaster, was put in charge of the cold buffet meal for the five of our corner, still friendly, in spite of passing coolnesses and "feelings" during the two years, four months and eight days of painfully close association. Our *plat de jour* was a huge platter, of an elegance unsurpassed even at the Ritz of Hormel ham, sausages and corned beef, sliced up and decorated with green beans, tomatoes and onion rings. A bowl of potato salad with real mayonaisse. The second of the long-hoarded tins of Mr. Delmonte's fruit salad, and then coffee, so strong that you could stand your spoon in it, with Klim made to the consistency of cream, and all the sugar we wanted. What a meal!!! We ate it out of doors, just by my garden patch, under Irene's striped garden umbrella and, if you didn't look at the washing lines, you MIGHT have been in any open air restaurant.

In the afternoon, we had a little uneasy see-sawing, especially when we saw the old "sewing machines" (the Japanese planes) going up for their afternoon stunts. But all the time, rumours continued to pour in, and passers-by kept calling through the fence that the news is true.

Then after the evening meal news ran around the camp that the Commandant would make an official statement. So we all gathered in and around F block, in the steamingly hot, but miraculously beautiful evening, and we stood and stood, on our poor flat feet, but there was no sign of the Commandant. At last our Representative appeared, and recited, in an expressionless voice, "I am sorry, but I have no good news for you. The Japanese put forward proposals to the Allies, and it will take some days for them to be considered. Meanwhile, fighting is going on, and camp life will continue as usual." But if ever a man didn't believe what he was saying, and if ever a crowd politely "played ball," it was then.

And now, as I am writing, the villagers are showing their joy by letting off volleys of firecrackers. So I think we are quite right in concluding that the little speech was dictated to him by the Commandant, a final face-saving gesture.

In the "Now It Can Be Told Dept." one may write that the very efficient short wave radio, that has all along kept us so well informed, was located in the brick stove used by our two "Farmers" and kept in the Farm building, in a direct line, not fifty yards from the Commandant's bungalow. He was constantly in and out of the Farm, and indeed the Farmers were often enough criticized for being unnecessarily matey with him! The Japanese have searched everywhere for the machine, and of late, with so many momentous discussions afoot, have, in self-defence, just switched off the power.

The latest bulletin is that San Francisco has broadcast that our terms have been accepted, excepting for some fine points as to who shall be in a government which will be agreeable to us, and whether we can leave them their Emperor, as consolation. Our Commandant has just sent round a message saying that camp life will continue as usual, until Allied authorities arrive to take over.

Oh, it is glorious and unbelievable, to think of life beginning all over again, and that, within measurable time, I shall hear from you again, and then see you again.

AUGUST 13TH. What a day of anticlimax! Confused and contradictory rumours pour in all the time. One moment the war is definitely over, the next it is irrefutably proved that fighting is still going on. So I just give up.

But worse than this, last night a drunken orgy and disgraceful exhibition of rowdyism towards the Commandant, who himself went to take roll call in the men's block, after asking their permission, culminated in the escape of two of the "celebraters" — if you can call them that. So if the war is not over, they certainly, and ourselves probably, will be punished. The Japanese here have behaved with admirable restraint and dignity so far — but there we are.

The very latest news — hot off the grill, is that Japan has been given twenty-four hours to say yes or no with "atomic" bombings going on in the meantime. Poor devils! I can't help it. It is quite easy to be magnanimous when one has won.

We are on tenterhooks. I have been called the hoodoo, because in an effort to relieve my restlessness, I have spent part of the past twenty-four hours in cleaning, sorting and recklessly throwing away, against that blessed day when I can leave — dear knows whether it will come in two days or two months.

A delightful, if apocryphal, notice alleged to be posted up in E block, makes one laugh, even on this day of bathos:

EXPERT PACKERS.
CHATTIES A SPECIALTY.

AUGUST 16TH. It was officially announced yesterday at 11:00 a.m. by Block Monitors: "Ladies and Gentlemen, the war is over." We had had unofficial messages and assurances some hours earlier, but we were a little cautious about accepting them after our disappointment of Monday.

By noon the Japanese had handed over the control of the camp to the Swiss Consulate. Union Jacks blossomed suddenly from the most surprising places, including the top of the water tower. Mail facilities started, radios are promised for today, and a messenger service to and from the Swiss Consulate.

130

In the afternoon we all got out our carefully hoarded respectable clothes, aired and pressed them, in preparation for the evening's Thanksgiving service and flag raising.

It was a short, but very moving service, held outside F block, and when the flags of the Allies were broken up on the roof, the atmosphere was electric with suppresed emotion. Even I, who am less thrilled than most over uniforms or flags, had cold shivers down the spine. Four years is a long time to have neither seen a friendly flag nor heard a friendly national anthem. I must add, that it seemed to me a blunder to play the old Imperial Russian one, but probably nobody knows the Internationale which I suppose would be the correct one for Soviet Russia.

After the service, the music lovers went up to F roof for the first time since the escapes of a year ago, and we had a gramaphone concert. Dancing on E roof. A beautifully cool moon and starlit night, which, with our new found liberty, made for delightful hours. In billets at 11:30 p.m., instead of 8:30 and none of us were tired even then.

Beginning today, we are to be allowed to go for walks in the surrounding countryside. I want to go alone, for the first time; it will be an extraordinary sensation, to go out of those gates after nearly two and a half years.

This morning the country people crowded round the fence and gates, with eggs, chickens, and melons for sale, or preferably, exchange for old clothes. Brisk bargaining went on, but prices soon became exorbitant, and my worn out rags stood no chance against the brand new "Dire Need" underwear that some reckless souls produced as payment.

The water cart went in to town for the usual water rations, but also laden with the first contingent of men going in to town, to the Consulate, or to see if their offices are still standing, or their homes. They will be back tonight.

LATER. As I was writing the last line, amidst the noise of a hutful of visitors, to my surprise and delight, I heard my name called, and there was T.S. standing. I don't think you ever knew him, but he has been my wise and untiring outside contact, sending in monthly parcels, and safeguarding the remaining valuables, jewellery, papers, etc. I wonder if you can imagine what it feels like to have talked with someone from the outside world, and especially one so full of helpful plans about getting me out of this place just as soon as official permission to leave camp is given. Any kind of accommodation is almost impossible to find, and with the collapsed currency, prices are fantastic. And I must confess to you, that though I am longing to get out of this place, I am suddenly terrified, afraid that I shan't have enough money, and what'll I do if I can't get away to some country where I imagine I still have some, and what — and what — etc., etc. My mind goes round and round. It is maddening to be suddenly so dithery, but I suppose it is an effect of being just a number for so long, where no decisions were in your power, and all you had to do was to obey.

AUGUST 23RD.   During the past week, it has been extraordinarily hard to keep one's mind upon camp duties, and yet we must all work in order to have meals, drinking water and for some sort of order to be kept in this community of seventeen hundred people. Very hard to instill this elementary rule of discipline upon a surprisingly large number of people who are resigning recklessly from their jobs or still worse, just not showing up for duty.

I must say, that of all the endings to internment that I had visualized I never pictured one anything like the actuality — something really worthy of a comic opera. But I might have known that it would have to be comic, being in China. The point is that for so long one has lost all sense of what country one was living in.

In the past week, we have been overwhelmed with visitors, both friends and strangers, so the noise, during daylight hours is beyond belief. We have been inundated with presents of food and money. Speaking of the former, my next but one neighbour has six cream cakes lying on her bed and nowhere else to put them, all presents from Chinese friends! And when it comes to money, we speak lightly of the $100,000 each that has been given us by a group of wealthy Chinese and tomorrow a further donation of half a million each. It was a very kindly thought, and I can't tell you what a pleasure it is to have some money of one's own again, to spend on something you would like to have but probably could do without!

Speaking of this, I amuse myself by speculating as to whether one can arrive at a good judgment of people's temperaments and characters by what they spend their money on, and by their pet and private economies. Some have turned just to food, especially chickens and butter. Others spend every cent on alcohol. Others to new clothes and frequent journeys to town. Others only want ice cream. For myself I turned passionately towards fresh fruit, some eau de cologne — and a permanent wave. Yes, we have even had a hair dresser come to the camp, and she attends us in our cubicles and gives machineless Perms! Price $170,000. So in order to afford these luxuries, I walk untold distances so as to save bus fares all the way to and from the town!

The Youth Association today presented each of us with a towel or handkerchief and most delightful gesture, the local guerilla general has sent his felicitations and together with sweets and cigarettes!

The Swiss Consulate and community have given lavishly of food, and on every side you see visitors bearing presents of fruit, cakes, chickens, sweets, eggs, beer and tinned food in such quantities that we can neither eat any more nor find anywhere to store it.

With mail and telephone established, inter-camp visits, trips to town (in charcoal driven lorries), country walks, cinema shows and dances, and Chinese labour to assist in camp duties, all show how we are gradually emerging from our limbo of internment.

Yesterday the advance party of doctors and businessmen left camp for good. They are hoping to be able, by occupation, to save their offices and homes from being looted, during this interregnum period between Japanese giving up control and Allied authorities taking over.

The weather is glorious, and one feels rather the same as one used to at the end of a rather uncomfortable summer holiday, whether in the mountains or by the sea. Won't it be grand to get home again?!

I am all packed up, except for bedding. To my great surprise, even our passports have been returned. Now I am only waiting for official permission to leave camp, as soon as I get that, T.S. is coming with a lorry to fetch me and my bundles. I am leaving it to him where myself and them are to be deposited!

AUGUST 28TH. The first batch of air mail letters for overseas left yesterday, as promised by the American Mission who visited us the day before. By it, I sent you the first proper letter I have been able to write in all these years. You don't know what is lying ahead of you, in the way of letter reading, when you will have to sit down and read this two and a half year old one.

One of the most interesting events, because it gave us a vivid idea of how modern armies are supplied by air, was the dropping by parachutes of American food parcels. (I hate to have to add, that there were the usual exhibitions of greed and "feelings" over the shareouts.) It was a beautiful sight to watch the great B29s roaring over the camp, low enough for us to see the hatch being opened, and the parcels being thrown, and the red, yellow and green parachutes opening like some fabulous flowers — as pretty as a giant's firework display.

An ironic commentary has to be added to the above. At one of the other camps, a Chinese woman was killed by being hit with one of the containers, their library building was wrecked, and here, considerable damage was done to crops with villagers and camp inmates alike churning over the fields in an effort to get to the parcels first. In short a good deal of harm resulted from a very kindly gesture. It is reported that when the Powers That Be, in charge of the whole operation, were approached with the meek suggestion that after all it might be wiser to deliver the very generous gifts by lorry, the answer was "Well, we can't deprive the boys of their fun." And this was not said as a joke.

Two days ago I took my Timmy to his new home in Hungjao, an adventurous journey on the truck that was transporting the farm animals to their new homes. Life is very lonely without him — in general it is much easier to say good-bye to two-footed companions than to four-footed ones! But really he had such endearing ways — to me alone — hiding in the grass and then jumping out at me, or following me as far as his courage would permit when I went to the pond for water, then hiding in a bush until I returned, then springing out and leading the way home. And he was always at the small bridge, waiting to welcome me home, when I came off duty from the hospital kitchen. I daresay the little blue saucepan had something to do with it, but he was a very charming cat. This morning I walked over to his new home to see how he was settling down — and he is lucky to have such dear people to look after him with a lovely garden. I found him bored with the comforts of near-civilization, and though eating well — a camp rule — always eat, and keep your strength up, you never know what is going to happen — he was crying for me and for the camp life he loved so well!

We have had another donation of pocket money, but it doesn't go far, with having to pay $35,000 for a lb of peaches, the same for an ice cream and $20,000 for the bus fare to and from Shanghai.

A delightful present/advertisement arrived today; a loaf of WHITE bread for each person, and on the wrapper:

I was feeling dreadfully restless and tired, and longing to be away from all this, and to be alone and quiet. Though I do realize the sense in waiting until official permission is forthcoming, especially as one can't get on with the picking up of pieces outside until banks and offices are able to function in some sort of way. And even the $15 million or so (to think that one was once a millionaire!) remaining from the jewellery T.S. sold for me, won't last long at the rate of $500,000 a day, which is what hotels now charge IF you can get a room!

AUGUST 30TH. Today's presents: (all from strangers or various Chinese charitable organizations). Toothbrushes, toothpaste, tea, potatoes, eggs, beer, envelopes, onions.

I write this truthful nonsense, to cover up the fact that I am almost sick with excitement. T.S. paid me another visit and has fixed up to come for me and my belongings on the 10th September, and he has got me a room in a private Chinese hospital. The reason for the hospital is because there is no chance of a hotel room, and as he explained, at the hospital I shall be well fed (the hotel rates do not include food) and all for $15,000,000 a month. Officially I shall go there suffering from anaemia and tiredness — both true enough. But of course the truth really is that one of his relatives is a doctor there, and as we know, in China, the fact of having a friend or relative established in any spot, at once removes all obstacles.

Faithful Li was waiting on the hospital steps with The Bicycle (polished and shining) which, under incredible difficulties, he had kept safely for me all these years — a basket of oranges with the usual congratulatory messages inscribed in black characters on red paper.

Ah Ching was there too — looking pretty and well, with a nice husband (he has a job in the Hongkong and S'hai Banking Corp. — so naturally knew to a cent the state of my finances), and a 6-month-old daughter, who was ceremonially "given" to me. All I could bequeath to her was the name "Victoria," and a rather pathetic antique brooch (coral and pearl crescent) not having any cash at all — and the last scrap of the famous Gold Bar which T. S. Yieh had bought with the jewellery I left with him in 1943 had to last until the rumoured evacuation ship arrived.

135

SEPTEMBER 12TH. The so-much-longed-for day, the day that one could hardly believe would ever come, came at last. I left camp two days ago, after two years, five months and five days. T.S. brought me straight to this small hospital and I am more thankful than I can say for this entr'acte of solitude, quietness and freedom from the daily chores.

The "corner" gave me a touching farewell meal and send-off. All my unpackable and unwanted possessions being appropriated before the corpse was cold, so to speak. The "corner" inhabitants were a very nice lot, and if we did try each other at times, we got along pretty well under almost impossibly trying conditions. If at times there was brutal frankness, there was always great practical kindness whenever it was needed.

And now all that is past, a unique experience in a lifetime, I should hope — something I am not sorry to have lived through, but which I am mortally glad to be finished with. Even after two days, those years are beginning to assume the vague incoherence of a dream, with the humorous element emerging rather more clearly than the rest.

From now on I shall firmly believe that the age of miracles is not past. To think that two days ago I was in the midst of all that noise and squalor, which spells "internment" and here I am, in this small but pleasant room, by myself. Oh! the indescribable peace and relief to be able to shut the door and be quite alone. A gloriously comfortable bed — and someone to make it for me. A medicine cupboard, with a mirror, and a basin with running water — that runs all the time, so that dressing and undressing is a delightful and leisurely performance, with one's toilet accessories all to hand. And how shall I describe the heavenly sensations of silk pyjamas and dressing gown, fresh brewed coffee and milk at 6:30 a.m. after hours of dreamless sleep. And freedom to go out and come in at will — even a tram ride is delightful.

The joke is that they feed me every three hours, take my temperature night and morning, and tenderly enquire after the works. All this the subject of ribald mirth from members of the "corner" who came to visit me yesterday that I should finish my camp career in hospital, I, who had escaped malaria, dysentery, the worst effects of malnutrition, chilblains and frostbite, septic sores and tooth troubles, and whose major affliction was obesity!

Well, that is all on the surface, underneath I need re-education for a return to a normal, individual life. When it comes to making

136

any decision, I feel like a child that has been given a problem far and away beyond its capabilities. I mull over and over the facts — quite simple ones really, with a thumping heart and a tummy gone to glory — and I get nowhere. I think that this is the worst effect of these years of being herded together and ordered around — just a number. T.S.'s quasi-humorous wisdom and active kindness are of great help during this transition period.

There are many confused rumours running around the town on the subject of repatriation ships. Each day I go the round of likely offices or consulates, usually come home with still more confused, vague and contradictory reports. But the most encouraging rumour was that there definitely will be a boat crossing the Pacific in a week or two, followed by at least another one some time next month.

The U.S.S. *Lavaca* arrived October 12th bringing back all the surviving internees from North China, including the "Haiphong Rd. prisoners." I was able to meet John at the Hongkew wharf and while he and fellow prisoners and their pitiful bundles were put into U.S. cars and trucks, cycled back to the Palace Hotel where I have been of help in getting him a room. It was a short and more moving reunion than I expected — but that is part of quite another story.

The *Lavaca* sailed next morning with the various remnants from the Shanghai Civil Assembly centres — including myself. My last evening in S'hai was spent in a typically touching Chinese manner. Li, Ah Ching and husband and his family entertained me at a lavish Chinese banquet in a celebrated local restaurant — I cycled there, and at the end of the celebration, Li and son-in-law ordered a rickshaw for me — gave the man the address of my hospital, paid him the correct amount and tip (after much arguing, naturally) and he delivered me "home" safely. Looking back upon this small episode of nearly 35 years ago — how "safe" we were on the streets at night in spite of all the horrors of war, under which the city and its Chinese population had lived during the previous years. Now, in 1980, in almost any country I would not feel so secure.

Next morning, Li was at the hospital at 6:00 a.m., summoned another rickshaw, paid and tipped him for the journey to the *Lavaca* — all I could give that great-hearted man in return was "The Bicycle" and the contents of my purse — a few hundred dollars of the debased currency, worth perhaps 20(?) cents in "proper" money.

PROCLAMATIONS

JAPANESE TO KEEP ORDER

WHEREAS being compelled by the state of war which has arisen between Japan on one hand and the United States of America and the British Empire on the other, detachments of the Japanese Army and Navy shall be as from today dispatched in the International Settlement for the suppression of hostile activities and for the maintenance of peace and order in the area, and

WHEREAS, however, the Japanese Military Authorities, whose first concern in taking this measure is the maintenance of peace and order and preservation of the prosperity of the Settlement, are ready to respect the life and property of the general public, even in case of nationals of the enemy countries unless either they act against the interests of the Japanese forces or their property is liable to hostile usage.

THE PUBLIC ARE HEREBY URGED that they will rest assured with the above intention of the Japanese Military Authorities and pursue their daily work as usual.

IT IS ALSO PROCLAIMED that those who act to the detriment of the general peace and order or in the enemy's interests, particularly those who act in contravention of the Japanese Military Regulations, and those who destroy or cause any damage to the public institutions or the stocks of essential materials shall be strictly punished in accordance with the Military Regulations.

COMMANDERS-IN-CHIEF OF THE
JAPANESE ARMY AND NAVY
IN THE SHANGHAI AREA

141

GENDARMERIE CONTROL

It is hereby proclaimed that:

I. The citizen of the United States of America and the subject of the British Empire, residing in the Shanghai area not less than fourteen years of age, shall be required

(1) To obtain permission from the Japanese Gendarmerie before moving his or her residence.

(2) To report to the Japanese Gendarmerie the following items (form available at the Gendarmerie Station), within five days here-after, and in person so far as possible, submitting at the same time three passport photographs, or, if such a photograph is unavailable, an autographed piece of paper (2" x 3") with the fingerprint of the thumb.

- a. Name
  Nationality
  Date of Birth
  Sex
  Status in military service
- b. Address (and telephone number)
- c. Occupation
  Kind of work (or position)
  Place of employment (name and address)
- d. Arms, photographic apparatus, wireless transmitter, motor-car and motor-cycle (Kind, make, number, registration or licence number, and other particulars).
- e. Real estate (Kind, locality, estimated value).
- f. Personal property not less than Sh. $10,000 in estimated value (Kind, locality, estimated value).
- g. In case real estate under (e) or personal property under (f) having been transferred within the previous five months, its kind, locality, estimated value, the name and address of the transferee, the date, price and reason of transferring.

II. If a citizen of the United States of America or a subject of the British Empire residing in the Shanghai area,

- (i) moves his or her residence hereafter without permission in violation of I - (1), or
- (ii) fails to submit a report under I - (2), anyone who knows of such an instance shall immediately inform the Japanese Gendarmerie. Anyone who is in a position to have known of such an instance and yet fails to inform shall be liable to severe punishment.

THE HIGH COMMAND OF THE JAPANESE FORCES
IN THE SHANGHAI AREA.